Dumpster Diving

DUMPSTER DIVING

Finding Treasure
in the Discarded Moments

BY LORI KLICKMAN

Xulon Press

Xulon Press
2301 Lucien Way #415
Maitland, FL 32751
407.339.4217
www.xulonpress.com

Requests for information should be addressed to:
Lori Klickman
29940 S 592 Lane
Grove, OK 74344
Outsideofordinary.lori@gmail.com

Printed in the United States of America.

ISBN-13: 9781545630884

Dedicated to my Mom, who taught me to laugh

in the midst of my struggles.

"I confess! I am guilty! Yes, I did encourage Lori to write. As you read this book, you will understand why. Lori Klickman is very creative in the little things of life, she not only sees humor, she sees God at work. Hopefully, after reading this book, you will look for the lessons God is teaching you in the little things of life and realize that God is in the details of your life.

Dr. Wayne Shaw – Oklahoma State Senator

"Lord, I want to be passionate and tenacious in my walk with you. I not only want to discover your many treasures, but I want to share them with others." – What a wonderful quote from this amazing book. This is just one of the many hidden treasures within this book. I truly enjoyed every moment that I spent deep in thought as I read each page. You will love reading this book from cover to cover. Lori is an excellent writer. Enjoy each chapter, as you are"

"Finding Treasures in the Discarded Moments." Donna Riley – Pastor's Wife and Mother of 6

"Lori Klickman has written a luminous, laugh-out-loud, faith based book that takes us through some hilarious episodes in her life. She has quite a unique ability to use the outcome of each event as a step to enrich her beliefs. This is a must read for anyone who believes that their God has a sense of humor."

Ron Young – Entertainer and Author
(The Only Boy Who Danced;
Author House 2011)

"Forged in the crucible of real life comes the pure gold of Lori Klickman's new book, **Dumpster Diving**. Hilarious, poignant, messy and meaningful, Lori's snapshots of real-life faith make this wonderful book the daily dose of encouragement we all need. Her honesty, vulnerability, quirkiness, sarcasm, truth-telling, timing and irony make this book a treasure chest of hope, trust and love. Don't buy this book if you want to stay in a bad mood, because your bad mood doesn't stand a chance. But, if you want your faith strengthened, your confidence boosted and your spirit energized, then by all means, pick up **Dumpster Diving** right now. You'll be glad you did.

– Tom Clegg, Senior Partner, The Clegg Consulting Group, Des
Moines, Iowa
(Author of Lost in America; Group Publishing 2001 and Missing
in America;
Group Publishing 2007)

"All of us could benefit from setting aside time to study God's Word as we grow in our relationship with Jesus Christ. Author/speaker Lori Klickman's refreshing and thought-provoking essays can enrich those devotional moments and I applaud her for making her creative words available to a wider audience."

– *Margery Kisby Warder, Christian Author. (Leaves that Did Not Wither;*

Parson's Creek Press 2013 and Elisabeth's Prodigal; Parson's Creek Press 2015)

Preface

Years ago my husband Keith discovered that people occasionally threw what he deemed "valuable items" into our local dumpster. Much to my children's embarrassment, he began bringing these treasures home. Most were eventually re-tossed, but I still have an absolutely beautiful room divider that is a one-of-a-kind piece. Years later I received a phone call from my son who was overjoyed to report to his father that he discovered a living room set outside of the dumpsters at his college apartment. He was thrilled to have the furniture—I think it was his way of apologizing to his father for all the previous mockery.

One thing I've learned along the way is that there is a morsel of joy and wisdom in every situation if you dig deep enough. I hope you enjoy "diving" into my dumpster with me and discovering some of the lessons I've learned, the joys I've celebrated, and a few difficulties I've overcome. I hope you laugh a little and think a little. Most importantly, I pray that God touches your heart and you find encouragement and inspiration.

Introduction

*J*oy is a personal thing. It is reflective of your personality. Some might jump up and down when joyful. Others might turn up the corners of their mouth. Some might even cry. It's the whole half-full/half-empty philosophy. You will soon discover that I am a "half-full" gal and guess what...I'm married to a "half-empty" man. God likes to keep a pH balance.

So, I admit I can be a bit of a "Pollyanna" at times. Trust me, you definitely don't want me around if you have road rage. I've been known to make up excuses for other people's poor driving habits that will not only bring tears to your eyes but even make you want to follow them home and offer to help. Tailgaters might be trying to get to the hospital to see their parent take a last breath, or those driving too slow might be trying to get their vehicle to the repair shop while the check engine light is blinking like crazy and they're scared to death, and...well, you get the picture. So not only am I half-full, I'm desperately looking for ways to overflow.

Let's start at the beginning. I mean REALLY at the beginning: Genesis 1:26:

"God said, "Now we will make humans, and they will be like us."

Here's my perspective on that verse: I was made in the image of God—I like to laugh, so God must like to laugh...at least according to the GAL (gospel according to Lori version). Now, I truly don't mean to be disrespectful of the Word...quite the opposite really. When I refer to the GAL, I'm giving you fair warning that this is my twisted perspective of what could or could not be the truth. Now here's where the secret unfolds: Psalm 139:13:

"You are the one who put me together inside my mother's body, and I praise You because of the wonderful way you created me. Everything You do is marvelous—of this I have no doubt (Wouldn't this be a perfect scripture for our mirrors?). Nothing about me is hidden from You. I was SECRETLY woven together deep in the earth below. With Your own eyes, You saw my body being formed. Even before I was born, You had written in Your book everything I would do."

I firmly believe God created me (and you) for His pleasure. Not only does God laugh—I'm pretty confident I crack Him up. Sometimes I think I can even hear Him laughing. It's the only explanation of why I get into the situations I do. Crazy things happen to me, and then God reveals Himself to me. We have an understanding. I provide Him with entertainment, and He teaches me stuff. Let's dive in!

Table of Contents

Animal Menagerie

1

Psychotic Mange

*A*round the age of 12, I begged my mother for a dog of my own. At that time, we had a German Shepherd, but he was an outside dog and not real friendly. He was big, strong, and had no obedience skills. His favorite hobby was to carry a log around everywhere he went. When he took us for walks, he insisted on carrying the log with him. Everyone in the neighborhood was afraid of Bullet.

There are probably some lessons to be learned from Bullet, but I want to tell you about Cesar. Mom gave in and let me get a puppy. He was a pedigree White German Shepherd and the very first live thing for which I was ever responsible.

Being the youngest child, I was always the one "being taken care of." I wanted to raise Cesar to be obedient and loyal. I wanted a companion. A real pet—one that didn't scare the neighbors and actually listened to what I said. So Mom enrolled us both in obedience school. I think she was secretly hoping I might learn a thing or two as well. We did pretty well together. I liked practicing with him, and I was so very proud that he actually understood how to sit and heel and all sorts of fun stuff. I even entered him into a couple of shows, and we won a few ribbons. Cesar was obedient and a pretty good dog.

However, as Cesar got older, he began to get "hot spots." He would lose hair in areas of his coat and incessantly bite and gnaw at the spots, only making them worse. We tried all sorts of remedies and baths, but nothing really worked. His biggest problem was that he refused to stop chewing on himself.

My mom was convinced that Cesar had "the mange." The veterinarian's response was, "He doesn't have mange, he only thinks he does." And I replied, "So he's psychotic," and from then on, the family agreed that Cesar had psychotic mange. Cesar was so convinced he had mange, he went on to chew himself so profusely we had to put him down. It was a sad and senseless ending for such a beautiful dog.

Have you ever been so deceived that you've sabotaged yourself? Someone told you that you were fat, and now you can't get thin enough? Someone laughed at you for whatever reason, and now you refuse to engage? You blew it so bad, that even though you know you're forgiven, you're convinced God could never use you for His ministry again, so you decide to stay home?

The devil loves to use our own mind to keep us from living the abundant life that God has for us. If you are bound by anything:

bad habits, shame, fear, grief...whatever has you in its chains, then you are not living the abundant life.

We dwell on the pain, and it steals the life from us. We believe the lie that it will never get better, and we gnaw. We turn our backs to the light, and we gnaw. We stop looking for help and we gnaw. We are sore, we are raw, and we are crippled by the deceit.

But what if we looked up and reached out for the truth? In the truth we will find that:

- we are made new and are enough through Him
- we have what we need in Him
- our very life is for Him.

Jesus told the people who had faith in Him,

> "If you keep on obeying what I have said, you will know the truth, and the truth will set you free." John 8:31

The lesson we can learn from Cesar:

> **—Deception can cause you to become your own worst enemy.**

2

Daisies & Frogs

*I*t all started with a Gerbera daisy and a good intention. I took a look at my potted daisy on the veranda and noticed the leaves were withered and it looked thirsty. I decided to bring the little guy into my kitchen and give him a haircut and a good soaking. I ran the water, and as I began to trim the leaves, I noticed an itty-bitty frog emerge from the dirt and hop out. He was cute as all get out, but I'm still not partial to slimy, hopping critters, so I was slightly startled as it jumped onto my kitchen counter. I grabbed the first thing I could find (which was my husband, Keith's favorite drink mug sitting by the sink) and quickly put it over the frog. Hmmmm...now what? Well, I thought, "Keith should be home shortly, and I'll let him "save" the frog and put him back outside. Surely the frog will live under the mug until then." The daisy remained in the sink, and I left the room. When I returned a few minutes later, I noticed a little frog hopping across my kitchen floor. I looked at the mug. It hadn't moved, and I quickly assessed that I had ANOTHER frog living in my daisy.

This little critter was more adventurous than the last, hopping around my kitchen. I contemplated just letting him go but then considered when he might reappear and where?—probably in my bed or bathtub. So I grabbed a big plastic bowl and threw it on top of the frog. Wow! "This is a little crazy," I thought, "Wait till Keith comes home and finds out he gets to save two frogs."

I sat back down in my living room and soon realized I had forgotten my glass of water. I returned to the kitchen to grab it, and my heart about jumped out of my chest when I noticed a rather large frog on my counter. It was big enough for me to do the squealy dance. Definitely too big for a coffee mug...and the worst part was, when it saw me, it took a flying leap onto the floor. This resulted in a MAJOR squealy dance!

At this point my dog, Buster entered the room. "BUSTER, GET THE FROG!" Buster looked at me pathetically and said, in that special dog voice that only dog lovers can hear, "You don't want to touch it, but you want ME to put it in my mouth?" He rolled his eyes.

The frog hopped...I danced...Buster laughed. "Okay," I told myself, "I can deal with this, seriously." I danced my way to the laundry room and grabbed a bucket. The frog hopped...I threw the bucket...I missed. The frog hopped, I danced, closed my eyes, and plopped the bucket ON THE FROG...but its leg was sticking out, which made me dance more. Buster was now rolling on his back laughing; I stared at it for a while. The leg didn't move.

I seriously couldn't bring myself to move the bucket. Now I was mad at myself. What if there was no Keith? What if I were on my own? How would I handle this? I realized I would just call a braver friend—so much for independence.

I was now aware that it might be a good idea to get the Gerbera daisy out of the house. As I grabbed it, you got it—another frog was on the edge of the pot. I grabbed the dishtowel to cover the pot and get it outside, feeling oh so brave as I walked by the mug, the plastic bowl, and the bucket.

A few minutes later, Keith walked in the door, and I explained my plight, showed him my collection, and he spent the next few minutes catching frogs and putting them outside—by the Gerbera daisy because, well, that's just how sweet he is.

Let me share my new-found wisdom:

> **Don't bring things into your "house" that should stay in the world. They will eventually spawn little critters...like attitudes and compromises...which will make you dance around and do whatever to hide them and keep them under control. Keep the daisies outside.**

3

Under the Bed

"Taste and see that the Lord is good." Psalm 34:8 NIV

What's hiding under your bed? I remember my childhood friend, Mary Kay used to keep a jar of peanut butter under her bed. Both of us had some minor weight issues as children, and her mother was forever putting her (and often me) on a diet. The peanut butter was Mary Kay's standby stash. I actually discovered it one day when we were playing in her room. I'll never forget her nonchalant response, "A girl's gotta do what a girl's gotta do."

Under the bed can be a dangerous place. Things get lost there. Things get dusty there. Things are hidden there— sometimes things that aren't so good.

My craziest "under the bed story" concerns another family pet, Wheezer. I do not recommend ferrets as pets. Wheezer was not particularly friendly, nor was he in any way talented. My daughter, Grace would let him run around our house like the ferrets she saw on TV. But rather than being a cute family pet, he just made a lot of messes. Wheezer was crazy, destructive, and hyper, until one day when he wasn't. Wow! Is the little guy finally becoming pet worthy, or is something wrong with him? Another day passed and he was even more lethargic. A call to the vet told us that he might have eaten something that didn't agree with him. He usually only played in Grace's room, so the search began. It wasn't long before a half-eaten chocolate nut bar was found under her bed. Evidently her brother, Joel had thrown it at her days ago, and it had gotten lost. Grace felt so horrible, but the deed was done.

The next morning Grace checked on Wheezer and tried to console him, only to have him bite her—and it wasn't a nibble. He then appeared to be having some kind of seizure. Out of fear, I grabbed our big leather fireplace gloves and secured Wheezer as only a brave mother would do, and we rushed off to the vet.

The vet did not give Wheezer much hope and suggested we leave him for observation. She would let us know if his condition changed. I sent Grace on to school in tears, and I went to my office. A few hours later I got the call that Wheezer had passed away. The combination of the excessive amount of chocolate and the peanuts basically destroyed his intestines.

Our ferret blew up from eating a candy bar.

I think I could find a number of spiritual lessons in this story—this time I'm going let you "dive" for them, and I'm going to state the obvious:

Diet is important—junk food really can kill you.

4

Buford

Grace did not have much success with pets. But Buford was the saddest story of all. Unlike Wheezer, Buford was soft and cuddly—I liked Buford. Buford was a fluffy white rabbit that lived in a little hutch in our backyard. Grace would also let Buford out to play on the deck, and we would all enjoy watching him explore.

One morning, Buster, the best dog ever, woke Grace up with his whining and nudging. Grace knew something was wrong, and when she followed Buster, she found Buford's hutch overturned, the door open, and Buford gone. I suspected a neighborhood dog became too curious. We looked everywhere for Buford to no avail.

The next day Keith discovered a "portion" of Buford in the woods, and now we would have to share the dreaded news with Grace. We placed "Buford" in a plastic bag and left him on the deck. For some crazy reason I thought Grace might need to see Buford for closure. She was heartbroken when hearing the news and declined the opportunity for a final viewing. We left Buford on the deck with the intention of burying him the next day.

When I woke up the next morning, I looked out the back window and noticed something that looked like cotton all around the backyard. It just took a minute to register, but yes, it was Buford—sort of! Another animal apparently got into the plastic bag, and now "Buford" was spread rather thin. I shrieked and yelled for Keith to quickly come help me pick up "Buford" before Grace woke up. This was too much for our heartbroken daughter. Back in the bag Buford went. Whew! We had the memorial service that afternoon complete with a poem written by Grace.

Now remember, we only had a "portion" of Buford when this nightmare started. A few days after the memorial service, I opened my front door...and to my horror I saw Buford's head on our sidewalk. I am not kidding. I guess a neighborhood cat thought it might be a nice gesture?

"KEITH!!!!!!!!! GET RID OF IT BEFORE GRACE GETS HOME."

Keith quickly threw Buford's head deep into the woods and promised me that it was over.

...Until a few more days passed, and the little neighborhood boy told Grace he found Buford's head in the woods.

We sometimes think we can hide the pain, the hurt, a lie, a secret sin. But unless we confront it and deal with it in the proper manner—confessing it to God and repenting, it will show its ugly head again—and it could be more disturbing the second time around.

> *"There is nothing hidden that will not be made public.*
> *There is no secret that will not be well known."*
>
> *Mark 4:22*

5

Deliverance

"Lord, if You are willing, You can make me clean.
Jesus reached out His hand and touched the man.
"I am willing," He said, "Be clean!"

Luke 5:13 NIV

I actually like vacuuming. There's something very ther-
apeutic about sucking up the dirt and making things
look fresh and clean...as if they were never dirty. No one knows
what it looked like a few minutes ago. It almost makes you feel
mischievous. You can hide dirt, bugs, food crumbs, confetti—
the list is endless. I accidently pushed the vacuum boundaries
recently.

I was enjoying a quiet day home alone just cleaning and putting my house in order. I was vacuuming the tile floor in the
basement with the nozzle attachment. As I approached the
door to the outside, I decided to open the door and vacuum the
threshold. I was quite alarmed to find a snake slithering into my
house (remember the squealy dance?). My plan of defense was

to take the vacuum wand and scoop it back out the door. The problem was that the vacuum was still on and I vacuumed up the snake.

Now I have one of those bagless vacuum cleaners so you can see the dirt swirling around and, in this case, Slimy was going for quite a ride. I was afraid if I shut the vacuum cleaner off, he might slither back out, so I did what every normal woman would do. I kept it on and sent a group text to my sister, Cindy, Grace, and Rachel. Rachel is a lawyer and really smart. I texted: I JUST VACUUMED UP A SNAKE—WHAT DO I DO NOW?

All three of them wanted details rather than offering solutions, but finally we came to the consensus that shutting off the vacuum was a scary proposition. Keith was not going to be home for some time so it was finally decided to shut the vacuum cleaner off while holding the hose in an upward vertical position, then carry the vacuum outside and let it stay there until Keith came home.

When Hero Husband arrived, I explained that I had a little mini crisis that only he could remedy. I'm pretty sure his chest puffed out just a bit as he asked, "What do you need?" I told him the whole story and sent him outside. He took the vacuum out to the woods and carefully removed the canister. As he tossed out the dirt, Slimy slithered away. He was still alive! Squealy dance reprise.

We can cover up a lot of dirt in our lives. But as time passes our "canisters" can get pretty full and we need to be emptied. I am so grateful for my Savior. He sees my insides, all the stuff I would never show the world swirling around and around, and He still loves me. He waits for me to shut my motor off. Then, when I cry out in desperation because I don't want to carry the dirt around anymore...He empties my canister and washes me clean. The dirt is thrown where He no longer sees it, and I am made perfectly clean again. Jesus is my Deliverer, and He's your Deliverer—today.

That stuff you're hiding inside is more alive than you think.

6

Deliverance II

*I*t's an icy cold morning and, once again, I'm looking out the bathroom window admiring the backyard and the pond and...wait. What's that swirling in the water? Keith and I both watch the unusual sight for a bit before Keith decides to take a closer look. He quickly returns to the house to tell me it's a young squirrel and he looks like he's drowning. He rushes to get the fishing net from the garage and saves the helpless creature. He brings the drenched fellow up to the veranda. Now what?

It's way too cold outside for the squirrel to survive at this point as wet as he is. His little heart is pounding, and he looks close to giving up. If we can just warm him up and dry him off, he might make it. But where and how? Keith offers his suggestion of the garage, but I think it's still too cold in there. "How about a box in the house?" I suggest.

Hmmm...we both have to leave for work, so he will be unattended. What happens if he successfully revives while we're gone? We decide to place a box in the corner tub in the master bath. We'll close the door just in case. We arrange a soft bed for "Peanut" on a warm heating pad and cover him with a light blanket. I blow-dry him (on low) for a bit. He is not responsive. I don't think this is going to end well. We leave for work.

I come home for lunch assuming I'm going to find a dead Peanut. I carefully open the bathroom door and see that the box is still intact. I cautiously approach the tub to find Peanut staring at me. His heartbeat appears normal...he appears to have made a full recovery. That's great news, except now what do I do with him? He's still just "laying" there so maybe I can carry the box outside, and he can jump out when he's ready. I gently reach for the box, but at the first sensation of movement, Peanut jumps up and startles me. I drop the box, and Peanut is now out of the box and into the tub. I run out of the bathroom and shut the door. Peanut is little and the tub is deep. Perhaps he is still contained? I call Keith and find he isn't far from home. Hero Husband is on his way.

Keith arrives, dons the famous fireplace gloves, and gives me specific instructions: "I'm going in. DO NOT open the door until I tell you to, and then be ready to immediately open the bedroom door to the veranda."

He's in and, at first, I hear him talking gently to Peanut. "Come here little guy. Looks like you're doing just fine. Let's get you outside." I then hear indescribable squeals and a lot of banging.

"Are you okay?"

"Dog gone it. Come here you little varmint." Squeal. Bang. Crash. "I got him…OPEN THE DOOR."

I obey, and Keith comes running out with the squirrel haphazardly held between the fireplace gloves. Keith heads out the second door. Once he gets outside, he tries to let go of Peanut, but Peanut is scared and scampers up Keith's arm. He attaches himself to Keith's back. Keith cries out. I reach for the broom, but Keith, in a panic, just grabs poor Peanut and throws him. He lands spread eagle on the side of the house. We run back inside and watch. Peanut just stays there. Maybe he's doing what people are supposed to do under those circumstances: remain calm and slowly check to see if I can move without doing more harm.

He was gone when we checked after lunch. Oh my. What an adventure. He was so helpless, so cute. Who would have guessed he could significantly traumatize my Hero Husband?

A choice can be like that. It can seem so insignificant. Maybe not the "best" choice, but it's so fun, or it tastes so good, or it's just what you need at this moment. But have you noticed that a choice can compound on you? And if it's a bad choice, the interest isn't always worth the investment. You may even have the best intentions in the beginning, but before you know it, the rascal has attached itself to your life and it's out of control.

"They sow the wind and reap the whirlwind."
Hosea 8:7 NIV

We all make mistakes, but sometimes we just knowingly make bad choices that eventually get us into a lot of trouble.

The same God that empties out "canisters of dirt" can get the squirrel off your back.

7

Flicka

*A*lmost every adolescent girl wants a horse. I was no different except that when I asked for one, I actually got one. My sister Pat, who already had several horses, offered to help my parents find one for me and also offered to provide a place for the horse to stay. You can imagine my delight when I was told my horse had been found and we were going out to a farm to meet her.

Her name was Flicka, and she was a 3-year old chestnut brown filly with a black mane, black socks, and a black stripe down her nose. She was beautiful and she was scared. Flicka had been hit by a car and was now very skittish. She probably wasn't the best choice for a novice rider, but the owners and my sister seemed to think we could overcome our inexperience and fears together.

There were no trails where I kept Flicka, so all of our riding was done in the pasture or on country roads. Roads that had cars, trucks, motorcycles, and bikes with bright orange flags— all of which terrified Flicka and would cause her to bolt, dance, jump—well, you name it. So when a vehicle would approach from either direction, I would grab on and pray, not knowing which direction I would be going in the next minute or if I would even be *on* a horse in the next minute, and I'm sure Flicka sensed my fear on top of her fear and, well, it wasn't pleasant for either of us.

She eventually learned to tolerate most vehicles, but she never accepted the bicycles with bright orange flags. We had some dramatic experiences before things started getting better. The worst was while riding next to a golf course. I honestly never knew what spooked her, but she bolted and took off through the golf course, making a mess out of the greens. Oops. And being the responsible adolescent that I was, I just went home.

The good news is that things did get better. She became familiar with the sounds on the road, and I became more confident in my riding skills. We grew to trust each other. We grew to love each other. I learned that she liked Twinkies and Texas sheet cake, and she learned that it really annoyed me when she would knock my hat off my head. She put up with me when I decided she should learn to jump over high fences. She decided to teach me that it wasn't a good idea—ouch! Then there was "trick" riding when she allowed me to hang from my saddle or stand on her back. It was not a surprise that all that "bolting" had made Flicka fast or that we went on to take third place in barrel racing at the Winnebago County Fair. We even won a first-place ribbon in Pleasure Class.

I spent almost every weekend and some weeknights with Flicka. She was honestly my best friend. But as I grew older, I discovered other activities, which included hanging with the girls and boyfriends. I started spending less time with Flicka. I felt bad and often would literally make myself go and ride so my parents didn't think I didn't appreciate my horse. Truth be told, as much as I loved Flicka, I wasn't really into riding anymore.

And then the telephone rang. I picked up the phone the same time my Mom did, and I recognized the voice of the owner of the stable, so I just listened. She informed my mom that Flicka was found dead in the pasture that morning. I threw the phone at the window and came unglued. I felt as though the floor in my life had given way, and I did not know how to cope with the startling news. No one close to me had ever died before.

I mourned for a long time. I wrote poems and listened to sad songs. I looked at her pictures, and I berated myself for not spending more time with her while I had her. But most importantly, I learned a very valuable life lesson: We will eventually lose everyone we love (at least on this side of eternity). People and animals are in our lives for a season, and in each of those seasons we grow a little more. Because of this, the time we have with them now is valuable, so we need to make the most of it.

I am so grateful for all the things that Flicka taught me. She made me brave, and I'd like to think that I made her brave too. Friends are like that.

"Some friends don't help, but a true friend is closer than your own family." Proverbs 18:24

8

Buster

*Y*ou've met Cesar—pedigree White German Shepherd. You've met Bullet, mostly German Shepherd and, rumor has it, part wolf. But you haven't officially met my favorite pet of all time, Buster. Buster was the dog that earlier alerted Grace to Buford's demise, but he was so much more than that.

Let's back way up. First let me say that Keith is not a "dog person." We attempted a puppy a few years previous to Buster. She was a Dalmatian named Oreo. She should have been called Humper, and we'll leave it at that. We gave her away.

We weren't even considering a dog when Buster found us. He followed Grace home one day while she was riding her bike. I took pity on the poor thing and fed him some leftover macaroni and cheese. He evidently thought that was pretty good fare, and he hung around our house for the next few days only to discover more delicious morsels from our fridge. Then we bought him some dog food, and then...we invited him into the house. We discovered that he was house trained and also that he was quite fearful if we raised our voices in any way. After much begging, Keith agreed that we could keep him, but he wanted nothing to do with him.

It was at that point we named him Buster and took him to the vet. She told us he was about 1 year old and showed some signs of abuse. She recommended we show him lots of love and patience, and he might just turn out to be the perfect pet. And that he did. Okay, maybe he wasn't "perfect." We did have to bail him out of doggy jail after he followed the Girls' Cross-Country Track Team into town.

We had Buster for 16 years. He played. He explored. He consoled a few broken hearts. He watched our children grow into adults and leave home. He watched Keith and I struggle through some marriage problems. He loved on the folks at Grandma's nursing home. He made friends with the neighbors. He would wait for me outside our house every day and dance with joy at my arrival. My neighbor, Donna would watch him when we traveled, and she reported that he would sit in the field a good part of the day watching for my car to come home. Through every life event he remained faithful.

We could all learn a lot from Buster. I couldn't write a book about all the outrageous animal stories in my life and not include a chapter on Buster. Everyone loved Buster. When he was in a coma and dying, many friends stopped by to pay their respects. He touched a lot of lives. Thanks to my Ya Ya Friends, Melinda,

Nan, and Benita, I have an evergreen tree in my backyard that continually reminds me of him. Buster had a few crazy moments of his own, and maybe someday I'll share those, but today I just want to honor him as The Best Pet I Ever Had. By the way, Mr. "I Don't Want Anything To Do With That Dog" cried pretty hard the day Buster passed. Love and loyalty can do that to a person. Thanks, Buster, for adopting us.

> *"Remember to welcome strangers, into your home.*
> *By doing this, some people have welcomed angels*
> *as guests without even knowing it." Hebrews 13:2*

Great Adventures

9

Lithuanian

I'm Lithuanian and very proud of it. My grandparents came over on the boat, or maybe it was my great-grand-parents. I'm not really sure—they all died before I was born. But either way, my father was 100% Lithuanian. Not that he spoke the language or anything. He just was. He was, however, a member of the Lithuanian Club, but I think the only requirement was to have wedding receptions and anniversary parties there or, at the very least, sit at the bar with other Lithuanians.

There are rumors (mostly in my immediate family) that I cannot admit or deny at this juncture, that I am Lithuanian royalty in exile due to the Russian takeover many years ago. On September 6, 1991, Lithuania was recognized as a free country again. I just stayed here—whatever.

Anyway, I love to tell people I'm Lithuanian. I mean, seriously, how many Lithuanians do YOU know? It makes me feel special. All this to say I had the most enlightening experience on one of our family vacations.

Keith and I took the kids on a cruise to celebrate their college graduations. One of the fascinating parts of a cruise is the international staff aboard. We were at dinner on the first night of the cruise, and one of the wait staff introduced herself to us and behold—SHE WAS FROM LITHUANIA. Oh my, you can imagine my excitement. I quickly proclaimed: "I'M LITHUANIAN TOO!!!"

The look on her face was priceless. I didn't know a look from a complete stranger could demoralize you so quickly. Somehow she managed to smile and yet proficiently convey that I was as Lithuanian as Fred Flintstone. The table went silent. My family knew that she had crushed me. She skipped off, and I looked at my distraught children and casually replied, "I don't think she was as excited about that as I was."

My mind raced. How could I prove to her that I was Lithuanian? I mean:

- I ate Kugili as a child
- I attended parties at the Lithuanian Club
- I rooted for the Lithuanian basketball team during the Olympics. (Once I even stayed up until 1:00 a.m. to watch them play the U.S. I cheered for them. I shed tears of joy when they won the bronze medal.)
- My brother was voted Lithuanian Father of the Year (dare I mention that they called him the day of the ceremony just to confirm that he was Lithuanian and did have children).

- I have a Lithuanian flag in my office

Okay, so that's all I got. Then it hit me. In reality...

I am a Lithuanian poser.

I had to face it. If I went to the Lithuania today, they would not recognize me as Lithuanian no matter how much I associate myself with Lithuania.

Jesus warned us of another time coming when many people will not be recognized regardless of how many times they were in church or associated themselves with Christianity.

> *"Not everyone who says to me, 'Lord, Lord" will enter the kingdom of heaven, but only the one who does the will of my Father who is in heaven. Many will say to me on that day 'Lord, Lord, did we not prophesy in your name and in your name drive out demons and in your name perform many miracles?' Then I will tell them plainly, "I never knew you."*
>
> *Matthew 7:21 NIV*

I don't know about you, but I do not want to stand before the Lord and try to convince Him that I am His. I want to see the look of recognition on His face, the look of an anxious parent welcoming their child home from war. When Joel returned home from Afghanistan, we all proudly waved our little flags as the troops marched in. I waved mine with so much vigor that the flag fell off and I was left with just a stick. That's the kind of welcome I want when Jesus sees me.

I love Jesus and I have made my confession of faith:

> *"So you will be saved, if you honestly say, 'Jesus is Lord,' and if you believe with all your heart that God raised him from death.."*
>
> *Romans 10:9*

Fortunately for us, we don't have to have been born in a certain place, speak a certain language, or celebrate certain customs. The only credential, and it's available to all of us, is that we need to recognize and believe Jesus Christ as our Lord and Savior, and we will be accepted into the kingdom.

> ***And who knows, maybe when I enter the throne room, Jesus will be waving a stick that used to be a Lithuanian flag.***

10

Overcoming

As I climbed the stairs, the voice in my head screamed, "YOU DON'T WANT TO DO THIS—THIS IS NOT GOOD— THIS IS NOT SAFE—WHY ARE YOU DOING THIS?" I was at Atlantis, a world-famous water park where the waterslides are in buildings and, well, you can't always see what they do or where they go...a feeling I'm not fond of. But this particular slide is famous. It's called The Leap of Faith. People come from all around the globe to have this experience. My kids wanted us to do this with them. We stood before the challenge and just stared. I reminded Keith that there weren't any ambulances at the bottom so we were probably going to be okay. We have to do this—we need to do this...for the kids. I only wish I had known exactly what I was committing to.

Are you like me? Do you like a little control in your environment—like knowing what's coming next and being able to prepare for it? I wonder if the disciples ever felt that way? Out of the twelve, at least one of them had to struggle with control issues. Jesus said,

"Follow me." Now, scripture doesn't spend a lot of time here, and it's evident that they followed Him, but don't you think at least one of them, at least in their head, was saying, "FOLLOW YOU WHERE? WHERE ARE WE GOING? WHAT'S GOING TO HAPPEN, AND AM I DRESSED APPROPRIATELY?"

I think about the original communion table. The disciples had followed Jesus for three years now. They'd experienced some pretty unpredictable moments, and every day brought a new adventure. From scripture we often see that Jesus didn't give a lot of details about what was going to happen. He gave just enough to let you know something was coming down. Go with me for a moment to the last supper. Jesus breaks bread, passes the cup, and then proclaims some pretty serious stuff:

> *Jesus said to his disciples, "All of you will reject me, as the Scriptures say, 'I will strike down the shepherd, and the sheep will be scattered.' " Mark 14:27-32*

Now let's go back to that one disciple. I don't know which one he is, I'm just saying the one that thinks, "NOW WHAT? CAN'T WE JUST HAVE DINNER WITHOUT ANY DRAMA? NOW WHAT'S HAPPENING? WHAT DOES THIS MEAN? I NEED MORE INFORMATION."

Okay, I'm being a little silly, but my point is that, from my perspective, it took a lot of faith to be a disciple—to follow Jesus when they weren't sure what the next day would bring or what would be asked of them or where they might end up. Very much like today. We don't always understand our circumstances or what God is doing in our lives, but we trust, we believe. He did everything He said He would do including dying on a cross for you and for me. He paid a huge price to guarantee He would get us where we need to be in the end. So when you feel like you're walking in darkness, know that He knows what's next.

There was a woman at the top of the waterslide just before me. She was more frightened than me. She didn't want to go down the slide, but she didn't want to walk away. She stood there frozen. I said, "Look at me. I'm old, and I'm afraid too, but I don't want to miss out on the adventure. I'll go next and you watch me." I got into position and looked at the red light. When it turned green, I would have to push myself into the hole where all I could see was blackness. I knew the young woman was watching me. I thought maybe I could influence her if I could just go for it. I can't let her down. I can't let my kids down. Green light, big breath, shut eyes and go...

DOWN A 120-FT DROP INTO A TUBE THAT GOES THRU A SHARK TANK!!!!!

When I emerged from the water into the sunshine, I screamed. Not with terror, but with joy, with victory. I overcame my fear, and at that very moment, I believed I could do anything. I went down every slide we could find that day. Hey, no sweat. After all, I survived the Leap of Faith!

> *Maybe that's the reason for the darkness—for the uncertainty. Faith will not only bring you back to the light but you'll be stronger...more resilient—and maybe even a little more joyful than before you took the leap.*

11

Blindsided

"The thief comes only to steal and kill and destroy;
I have come that they may have life, and have it to
the full." John 10:10 NIV

*H*ave you ever been so comfortable that you were unaware of danger right next to you? I know I have wondered how people walking down a track can get hit by a train. Did they not hear the train coming?

My husband and I were confidently toting our luggage down the platform towards our train. It's true we both realized we overpacked for our journey and wished we didn't have so much to carry. But that choice was in the past, so we were bearing our burdens, thankful for the opportunity to see new places.

Our train would take us to Munich, Germany, and we were consumed with the wonder of what new sights, tastes, and adventures lie ahead. I approached our car first. There was a man about to board, and he courteously motioned for me to go ahead. Being aware of the amount of luggage we needed to load, I declined his offer, but he kindly insisted which separated me from Keith. I waited to help Keith with our big bag, but I saw the kind gentleman helping him, so I moved on to find my seat. Keith was soon next to me, and we were on our way.

It was about 30 minutes into the journey when Keith realized his wallet was missing. Panic set in. I quickly blew off my commitment to avoid costly international calls and phoned our previous hotel in hopes the wallet was still in the room. No such luck. We recalled the events of the morning and spoke with another family member who boarded after us. It didn't take long to put the story together.

The kind gentleman who insisted I board was seen walking behind us, passing us, and waiting for us. As he "helped" Keith with the big suitcase, another man came alongside Keith and took his wallet. The men were seen walking away from the train rather than boarding it. We had been robbed. Our cash, of course, but also our credit cards and all of Keith's personal information was gone as well.

Before we could contact our bank, hundreds of dollars were drained from our account, and charges were made to our cards. We spent an additional hundred dollars in international phone calls. Being violated, whether physically, emotionally, or even financially, brings a helpless despair that causes one to yearn to be rescued.

I was angry, I was frustrated, and I felt so bad for Keith. I knew he felt foolish and somewhat at fault. How could someone do this to us? We were on vacation, and we were very, very far from home. We spent the next hour of our journey calling the bank and our credit card companies. Once we had all the accounts closed, we chose to try to forget about our misfortune and enjoy our trip. Fortunately I had a separate credit card in my wallet that we could use to obtain cash and take care of expenses for the remainder of the trip. We would be all right.

When we arrived home, we were forced to face the nightmare once again. We met with our banker and talked with our credit card companies. We surveyed the damage. We went through the process of getting new cards, a new driver's license for Keith, and filing a claim for identity restoration. What we discovered was that, outside of the cash in Keith's wallet and a large phone bill, everything could be restored. We're back to normal now. Our bank even restored the money stolen from our account (God bless that bank!) We will, however, have to keep an eye on our accounts and credit reports for many years to be sure someone isn't posing as Keith for a loan or a credit card.

The thief came. I could say he stole our money, he killed our joy, and he destroyed our vacation. That's what he set out to do. And maybe, for a few moments, it appeared he accomplished his goal. But then...we were rescued.

In this world, the thief comes often, and his attacks can be violent or subtle, but his purpose is the same: to steal, to kill, and to destroy. He attacks our families, he attacks our bodies, he attacks our finances, and he attacks our minds. However, His plan is always, and will always be, cut short because our God has come to give life—abundant life at that. Your rescue is imminent. It may not be tomorrow, but it is for sure.

> *"At night we may cry, but when morning comes, we will celebrate."*
>
> *Psalm 30:5*

What a glorious hope, what a peaceful promise.

12

Thirty-Eight Minutes

I love Jesus. He owns me and I am His. I gave Him my life many years ago. He is my Lord and Savior, and He is in control of my life...most of the time. Oops. Who am I kidding? I have control issues. I like my life tidy and intentional. Everything has its place in my home and in my life. I get very uncomfortable when it gets messed up for longer than twenty-four hours. I can get very crabby and dramatic. It's not pretty.

God recently turned the light on my control issues, and I learned a valuable lesson. I was preparing to fly to New York to see my daughter, Grace. I was choosing my flights, trying to get there as quickly as possible and spend as little money as possible. Most of the flights were running around $300.00, and then, lo and behold, I found one for $225.00. Eureka! The flight times worked perfectly with my schedule except for the short layover in Cincinnati.

I typically like to leave at least an hour between flights to avoid anxiety. It allows a threshold for a late departure and keeps things neat and tidy. This inexpensive flight only gave me forty-five minutes. Hmmmm. After some thought, I decided the Cincinnati airport can't be that big. Forty-five minutes should work just fine. What's a little adventure? I made the purchase and sent the itinerary to Grace.

A few days passed, and while talking to Grace, I mentioned how brave I was scheduling a connecting flight with only a 45-minute layover. There was a brief silence on the other end. Grace suggested that I take another look at my itinerary because yes, she was impressed with my bravery (knowing my anxiety issues), but I actually only had 38 minutes. WHAT?

It was true. I don't know how I missed it, but my layover was only 38 minutes which meant I really only had 23 minutes before the cabin door of my connecting flight would close and I would remain in Cincinnati for the rest of my vacation. My anxiety rose quickly and the battle began.

From that point I assured myself daily that God was in control of the situation. I chose to believe that this was a trust-building experience for me. After all, it's easy to trust God when you don't take any risks. This was going to be good for me. I found scriptures to build my faith, and I chose peace. Whether I made the flight or not, I would be where God wanted me to be.

Perhaps you think I'm being overly dramatic but, folks, this was a huge deal for me. These situations make me VERY nervous. I occasionally mentioned my situation to my friends (looking for affirmation), and every single one of them cast doubt that I would make the flight. That didn't help. It truly was a battle for me not to worry, especially as the day got closer and closer. I have missed flights before. I know the hassles. Please God, no.

I found myself awake in the middle of the night, so I began to formulate my plan for all the "what-ifs." What if I have to take a much later flight? I could find a nice restaurant and relax. What if there are no other flights that day? I could get a hotel room and get the earliest flight out. What if that flight is full? I had to have a plan so I could feel secure. Then I recalled an article I recently read that said if you bring chocolates for the flight attendants, they will be more apt to take care of your specific needs. So maybe, if I presented them with a gift, they would allow me to change seats to enable me to get off the plane faster and...and then I heard the voice in my spirit quietly say:

"I thought I was in control of this one."

I was humbled again and even slightly embarrassed. Did I actually think the God of the Universe truly needed my organizational and problem-solving skills to catch this flight? This was getting way out of control. I surrendered and went back to sleep, promising God that I would stop obsessing.

Departure day arrived and I entered the airport terminal one and one-half hours before my flight departure (just to be safe).

The man who checked my bags seemed so kind. I just couldn't help it, and I found myself explaining my 38-minute situation to him and asking him what my options were if I missed the flight (so much for trust). He looked at me with the kindest eyes and offered to look at my itinerary. He tapped on his keyboard and then again looked at me with those compassionate eyes and assured me that the airline would not book me on a flight I could not make. He gently told me I wasn't going to have any problem, everything was going to be just fine. And I believed him and thought just for a minute I saw a halo above his head. Why couldn't my friends tell me that?

My flight to Cincinnati departed a few minutes late, but the pilot assured us we would make up the time in the air. I relaxed and read my book. Every time my thoughts wandered to my connecting flight, I took a deep breath and quoted a scripture. Before I knew it we were landing. I took a deep breath and thanked God that He was in control.

I was seated in aisle five and I didn't have a carry-on to retrieve (I planned that). I just needed to move quickly and find the connecting flight board.

I am not going to stress. I got...err...God's got this!

"Surely your goodness and love will follow me."
Psalm 23:6 NIV

I just kept saying that in my mind, over and over again. The cabin door opened. We were five minutes late. I had eighteen minutes.

I was the first one to enter the terminal, and I could not find a connection board. I started running until I saw an attendant at another gate desk. I ran up and inquired, and she told me I was at Gate B25 and needed to get to Gate B10. That sounded doable, especially with the moving sidewalks. I huffed and puffed and, feeling more like Alice in Wonderland than the Big Bad Wolf, I ran down the longest corridor I have ever encountered. I stopped once to catch my breath, but my inner voice screamed, "If you don't keep running, you'll never make it. You will hate yourself for having to stop and rest when you miss the flight."

People stepped out of my way. I'm pretty sure I heard the angels cheering. I ran and ran, and finally I could make out the gate number ahead. Geez, it looked like another full city block to go.

As I finally approached Gate B10, I saw a phenomenal sight. There were people in line. They were getting ready to board. I wasn't too late! I made it! I got there just in time to hear the announcement:

"For those of you just arriving, we are delayed just a few minutes while we wait for our crew to arrive."

I laughed out loud. I'm pretty sure God was laughing too. "Smooth move, God." I had time to go to the bathroom and grab a snack. I sat down to finally catch my breath and wipe the sweat from my brow, and when I looked up, I noticed at least five other people who were on my previous flight just casually walking up to the gate.

Really?

13

The Bubble Bath

*S*edona, Arizona, is one of the most beautiful places I have ever been. I've been fortunate to visit several times but the last time was the most memorable. My nephew Ben-o was receiving his Master's Degree from Northern Arizona University, so several of the family members (Peter, Cindy, Penny, Roy and, of course, Keith and I) decided to convene in Sedona and attend the ceremony in Flagstaff. We rented a house near downtown with a lovely view of the Red Rocks.

On our first night there, Cindy surprised each of us with a gift of scented shower gel to make our vacation even more delightful. Other treats were distributed as well—special coffee, some unique snack foods, and a couple of bottles of wine. We were set to have a wonderful weekend together.

One of the amenities of our new digs was a hot tub in the backyard. We set aside an afternoon to snack on cheese and crackers and hang out in the tub, viewing the beautiful vistas of Sedona. A perfect day to be had by all.

Cindy was last to climb into the tub. As she entered she announced that just *maybe* someone's shower gel leaked in her suitcase because her swimsuit smelled unusually good. She plopped down into the water, and within seconds massive amounts of suds began forming around her and soon around us. The bubbles just kept growing and growing, and we kept laughing and laughing. A full-blown belly laugh, the kind where tears stream down your face and you can't breathe. Mounds of bubbles were everywhere! A helicopter flew over, and Peter signaled for help as he was sure it was sent to rescue us from the mounding bubbles now pouring on the grass—perhaps to arrest us for hot tub abuse. It's an adventure never to be forgotten in our family, but let's dig a little deeper.

I couldn't help but be reminded of the little boy with the loaves and the fishes. Scripture lays out the story of over 5000 people gathered to hear Jesus speak and, well, eventually people started getting hungry. The disciples thought the best course of action was to send everyone home but Jesus thought it would be more time efficient just to feed everyone right where they were. The disciples reminded Jesus they had no food (well, except for the kid with the five loaves and two fish). We all know the end of the story. Jesus took that small offering and fed everyone in attendance and still had twelve baskets of leftovers.

When we give what we have to God, He is always faithful to multiply it.

"Bring the entire ten percent into the storehouse,
so there will be food in my house. Then I will open
the windows of heaven and flood you with blessing
after blessing."

Malachi 3:10

Cindy brought her few drops of shower gel to our tub and, well, we all walked away a little cleaner, a lot happier...and even smelling a little better. Thanks for sharing, Cindy!

Hope the hot tub was okay.

14

The Valley of Death

"I may walk through valleys as dark as death, but I won't be afraid. You are with me." Psalm 23:4

*J*esus goes before me. Jesus goes beside me. Jesus goes behind me.

These are words I muttered over and over again during my trip through Europe. I was anxious before I departed, knowing I would be facing the physical challenges of keeping up with a "young" group, lots of walking and climbing in high temperatures, and new experiences. The day before my adventure, I stumbled on a devotional that talked of peace and used the words above in the final prayer. I have not been able to locate the original devotion, but the prayer has stuck with me to this day, so Lord, bless that person for saving my life.

Who wouldn't want to go on a bike tour of Paris? Sounds so enchanting—and it was, most of the time. My family of nine (Keith, Joel, Peter, Cindy, Rachel, Kyle, Sonny, Alex, and of course ME!) was given brief safety instructions from our guide. My very favorite was the command to DOMINATE—illustrated by the guide thrusting his fist into the air indicating that as a group we were to (literally) take over the road and subject all other vehicles to a lesson in patience. So, now well trained (ha, ha) and donning our florescent vests, we jumped on our metal steeds and headed down the lovely cobblestone street.

I don't really bike ride much, so I was completely relying on the "it's like riding a bike" adage. After a few initial wobbles, I found my confidence, sighed and took in the Eiffel Tower. Then we hit a busy street...a major street...did I mention we were in Paris? There I was, surrounded by cars, stoplights, buses, honking horns, other bicycles, motorcycles, and FEAR. Jesus, you go before me, beside me, and behind me.

I weaved, I wove, I slowed down, I sped up until, well, the stoplight turned red...and my family was all ahead of me, leaving me alone in a busy intersection in a foreign country—and they just kept riding!

The rest of the stragglers now looked to me as their new leader...seriously? The light turned green and off we went. So glad Jesus was there because I pedaled as fast as I could to catch up. Soon we were back with the group and headed down a welcomed side street where we stumbled upon a woman from a previous tour. She had fallen off her bike and was now bleeding. This was subsequent to seeing Joel run into a road barricade and previous to Peter zipping under a canopy only to hit his head on the frame. The guide encouraged us to hang in there...ice cream was in our future.

As the evening progressed and the sun began to set, we were all getting more proficient in our riding skills. The ice cream helped a lot too. The bridges, the Louvre, all of Paris blew by, and now we headed to the last leg of our journey, a boat cruise down the Seine.

It was at this point of the journey things got ugly. To get to the boat, we had to ride down a steep cobblestone hill. This hill would be a challenge on its own, but now add that it was completely full of slowly moving tour buses and cars. Our guide told us it looked more daunting than it actually was. He promised if we keep our eyes focused ahead, we can easily navigate the narrow path "just be aware of side mirrors." ARE YOU KIDDING ME? Everyone started following him single file, and then it was my turn.

Now, I'm no sissy and I'm certainly no quitter, but I was freaking out on the inside. All I could think about was the "Valley of the Shadow of Death." And so, I began my declaration: Jesus, you go before me, Jesus you go beside me, Jesus you go behind me, and Jesus, I hope you don't run into anyone or into any of these vehicles.

I made it, unscathed I might add. And...the cruise was the most enchanting part of the evening. Seeing the "City of Lights" from the river, seeing the people picnic and gather on the banks of the Seine, and viewing the Eiffel Tower, literally twinkling and celebrating my victory. Oh my!

I learned a few things in Paris that night:

- *Fear is just an obstacle;*
- *The valley always looks more daunting than it is;*
- *If I keep my eyes focused forward, I won't wobble nearly as much;*
- *The best part of the journey is on the other side of the valley.*

15

The Root Canal

Not long ago my front tooth began hurting, and before I knew it, I was scheduled for a root canal. Now, my only experience with root canals was listening to people use the experience for an analogy whenever they wanted to emphasize the worst possible event. I was pretty nervous going, even though several friends told me "it was no big deal." As I sat in the chair awaiting the procedure, I examined all the tools laid out and tried to figure out what was about to happen to me. From my perspective, comfort was not in my immediate future.

The dentist sat down by my side and immediately assured me that I would be okay as he approached my mouth with the "needle of numbness," causing a tear to run down my cheek. Within minutes my mouth was indeed numb and my sore tooth didn't hurt anymore. In fact, I found myself reaching to be sure my nose and lips were still there.

From that point on, I was amazed at how easy the procedure actually was. It honestly did not hurt a bit. The worst part was trying to keep my mouth open and the cramp in my foot—evidently root canals cause my feet to cramp? I found myself thinking, "Wow, this really was a piece of cake!"

...Until I got home and the numbness wore off. Then I was praising God for the pain pills even though they were not strong enough to mask my discomfort. The pain lasted for days. I even called the dentist to report that I was very uncomfortable and perhaps something went wrong. He told me to call back in a WEEK if I was still in pain. Seriously?

Over the next day or so, as I wallowed in my self-pity, I began to think about how our sinful choices are a lot like a root canal: At first you are numb to the consequences of the choice, and you firmly believe that it's no big deal. But then the pleasure wears off, and you're left with the results of someone drilling a hole in your tooth.

Don't let the world fool you. In the end, sin really hurts.

16

To Thai or Not to Thai

I love food, but I don't know Thai food. I never had Thai
food. Thai food sounds really spicy—I don't like spicy.
HOWEVER, while traveling with my extended family, I was over-
ruled, and they decided we were going out for Thai. They promised me I would find something I liked. Yikes!

As I perused the menu, I soon discovered that when you order
your food, you choose the level of "heat" with 5 being the spic-
iest. I could do this. I ordered chicken noodle soup (my family
made fun of me) at a heat level of 1.

My chicken noodle soup was very bland. Duh! I soon began
tasting everyone else's dishes to discover that I actually like a
little heat, and the unusual dishes were much tastier. So I learned
yet another lesson: When you stand on the edge of adventure,
you miss the REAL experience.

I can't think of a single man or woman in the Bible, who was
faithful to God, that did not take some sort of risk. I wonder
if some of us are living our Christian life at a level 1 heat and

wondering why our spiritual life is so unfulfilling? Maybe it's time to hang around some level 3, 4 or even 5 Christians and taste a spicier version. I certainly don't want to live so comfortably that I miss the faith adventure.

"But since you are lukewarm and neither cold nor hot,
I will spit you out of my mouth." Revelation 3:16 CEV

I'm turning up the heat!

17

Let Them Eat Cake

While traveling in Paris, I took on the challenge of leading some of my family members on a "Chocolate Walk" I discovered on the internet. We had a wonderful time exploring a neighborhood that housed many of the finest chocolatiers...quite an adventure! In the midst of all the chocolate, we stumbled on a boulangerie (bakery). It had the most beautiful desserts I have ever seen...I mean, seriously. The colors, the glazes, the swirls, the chocolate, the cream...you couldn't help but want to buy *something.* Food that beautiful just has to be tasted. I think of the intentions of the artisan baker who created, not only a decadent rich cake, but then decorated it to be sure it was enjoyed and experienced in the most satisfying way.

Now imagine buying one of those incredible desserts, bringing it home, and then just setting it on the shelf. You look at it occasionally, admire it...your friends admire it, but you never taste it. Then you read in a book about someone actually eating the cake, so you decide to do something a little crazy, and you take a bite of your cake. "MMMM…whoa, that's really good!" It might be the most incredible thing you ever tasted, but you put your fork down and never take another bite.

What a crazy scenario, right? Yes, this is what I thought of when I read James 1:22-25:

"Obey God's message! Don't fool yourselves by just listening to it. If you hear the message and don't obey it, you are like people who stare at themselves in a mirror and forget what they look like as soon as they leave. But you must never stop looking at the perfect law that sets you free. God will bless you in everything you do, if you listen and obey, and don't just hear and forget."

Going to church on Sunday, reading a chapter in your Bible, or even reading a devotional, and not applying it to your daily life—not living out the truth you hear, is not living an authentic Christian life. It certainly leaves you short of God's best for you. To be honest, I'm too vain to relate to looking in a mirror and forgetting what I looked like, but I can relate to the ridiculous idea of buying a mouth-watering cake and not tasting it or discovering how truly amazing it tastes but never taking another bite.

The Word of God is not only nice to read or listen to once a week. It is to be devoured. When applied daily it will seriously change your life. Hopefully it will even make you FAT: Faithful, Available, and Teachable.

So cut a big slice...and be sure to share with your friends!

18

One More Step

few years ago, I had the privilege of traveling to Italy with a group of crazy women, who either had or were soon to turn fifty that year. You can imagine the memories we made as we toured Tuscany, seeing the famous sites, meeting new friends, attending wine school, and enjoying as many new experiences as we could stuff into our journey. One of the "crazier" adventures happened on the night of our arrival.

As with any trip to Europe, the journey was long. We left from Tulsa, stopping in Chicago (where I met up with my sister Cindy, who hopped on our plane). We flew overnight to Frankfort, Germany, and then on to Florence, Italy. But before we could declare "arrived," we had yet to jump into our rented vehicles and find our way to our villa in Tuscany. Unfortunately it was much farther than any of us had hoped.

Hours later we drove up a gravel road and beheld the beautiful villa nestled in the vineyard-laden hills of Tuscany. At this point I was impressed by the panoramic moment, but my mind was recalling that our villa included meals prepared by the owners, AND I WAS HUNGRY. We opened the large wooden door to be greeted by our host family, a warm fire, and bottle of something delicious and bubbly. Within minutes we were toasting and chatting with our new friends as our first truly authentic Italian meal was being prepared for us.

Several courses later, and with very full stomachs, the exhaustion was catching up with all of us. Just when our eyes were focusing on our sleeping quarters, one of the young men from the family suggested we go to the hot springs bath house that he claimed "wasn't too far away" for a relaxing dip. Just about everyone laughed at the absurdity of leaving our warm and cozy new home, except of course, me, my sister, and two others...we wanted to know more. Who wouldn't want to experience an Italian hot spring bath on a cold spring evening? I didn't care how tired I was...I just couldn't imagine missing an adventure like that. So we grabbed our suits and let the locals lead the way.

"Not too far away" was about 45 minutes. Geez, I was tired and a wee bit nervous—not knowing what to expect. But it was so worth the trip. It was set up much like one of our public pools, including a locker room. There were several pools, indoor and outdoor—we gravitated to the house pool where we could behold the star-filled sky above from an Italian perspective. The hot mineral water felt amazing after the incredibly long journey. Relaxing in the pool and listening to the Italian chatter surrounding us,

Cindy and I just giggled. I looked up at the always amazing stars and said a little prayer of thanks. I felt so incredibly *blessed*.

However, reality kicked in reminding me there was still another 45-minute drive ahead of us before we could crawl into our beckoning Italian beds. Even though I think I could have fallen asleep standing up, I will never regret taking that "one more step." Nor will I forget how I found my sister when we finally arrived back at the villa—kneeling on the floor of the van, her head on the seat...asleep.

"Heaven and earth will praise our God and so will
the oceans and everything in them." Psalm 69:34

Thank you, Father, for your wondrous creation and the many blessings found in the adventures you lay before me!!

19

Where the Road Leads

$\mathcal{V}$acationing for control freaks (like me) can be exhausting. Although we take great pride in our planning and organizational skills, it takes a huge amount of effort and time to make sure every detail is addressed, every potential crisis prepared for. I cannot even count how many times I have uttered the words, "a real dream vacation would be one that someone else planned."

So I decided to step outside my circle of ordinary and go on a trip with only minimal plans. My husband and I purchased our round-trip airfare and scheduled a rental car. I perused the map of Maine, did a little research on interesting things to see, and well, that was about it. Let the games begin!

We arrived in Portland a day before our luggage (this could have been a disaster, but for someone with no plans, it simply meant an extra day seeing several lighthouses in the Portland area. Therefore, it was a great day, and the first "win" for spontaneity.

Once our luggage caught up with us, we took off up the coastal highway and stopped at the first information center we came upon. We had a great conversation with a gentleman who gave us our plan for the day. He suggested we drive down two of the most scenic peninsulas. Our trek began, and our first stop was a quaint roadside restaurant heralding "fresh clams." Now, I live in Oklahoma, and I think Mrs. Paul's fried claims are pretty darn good. Sorry Mrs. Paul, but you will forever be second rate from now on. Besides my delectable discovery of what fried clams are supposed to taste like, I asked the restaurant owner why her establishment was named *The Giant Steps Café* since there were no apparent "giant steps" in sight. She then told us of a nearby hiking trail that would lead to the actual "Giant Steps." Thirty minutes later we were standing on the breathtaking oceanside rock formation. Even I couldn't have planned a better day. But the adventure continued: We explored a lighthouse at Pemaquid Point. We were allowed to climb up and explore the working lighthouse as well as learn the different lighthouse signals. We then drove a little further and ate our first "lobstah" roll at a local lobster "pound"—a new concept for us. It's basically a very casual, walk-up-to-the-window, order, and sit-down-with-the-locals kind of place. We sat outside and literally watched the boats coming in and delivering the lobsters. Now that's fresh! Thank you, Mr. Information Guy! But now...where to sleep? I got on the internet while Keith drove north towards Rockland. We found a very comfortable inn and rested up for another big day of exploring. We did a little research and found a very curious Airbnb rental in Stonington, another harbor town at the very point of an upcoming peninsula. The owner of the establishment suggested we make time for a stop at the Penobscot Bridge on our journey.

We got an early start and headed toward Stonington. I read that the harbor town of Camden was not to be missed, and we soon discovered why. Outside of the spectacular post card views of the bay and the huge sailboats, the shops and restaurants were a delight. But the biggest surprise was Camden State Park—an easy drive up a mountain, resulting in a breathtaking view. Before long we were at the aforementioned Penobscot Bridge and discovered we could take an elevator to the top (over 400 feet), and you can only imagine THAT view. It is located about 5 miles from the mouth of the river. Simple as it was, the most fascinating thing I saw that day was a white line down the middle of the river as far I could see. I inquired of a guide who confirmed what I had suspected. The line was caused from the salt water of the ocean colliding with the fresh water of the river. Also located next to the bridge was the Fort Knox Historic Site. Now I'm not normally a history buff, but I enjoyed climbing around an actual fort that was used during the American Revolutionary War, imaging the battles fought for our freedom.

We arrived in Stonington at sunset, and after crossing a rather narrow suspension bridge, we found ourselves at the very tip of the peninsula. It felt like I was on the edge of the world. Little did I know that the next day I would experience the highlight of my Maine adventure:

It began with a morning walk in Stonington, a beautiful little harbor town known for its lobster industry as well as its granite excavation. While strolling through the sleepy town, we noticed a sign offering a one-hour seal tour for a very reasonable price. We inquired at the nearby jewelry merchant. She was a bit of a character, quite harried (reminding me a bit of the rabbit in the Winnie the Pooh stories). She explained to us that she was preparing for her annual move to Florida for the winter. However, as I perused her jewelry, she slowed down enough to sell me a beautiful bracelet. She promised that "Captain Steve" gave wonderful tours and encouraged us to book one. The only problem was she wasn't sure where he was and, well, there's no consistent cell service in Stonington. When she saw our disappointment, she "hopped" into her house, grabbed her land line phone, and produced the voice of Captain Steve on the other end. After very little conversation, we had a tour booked for later that morning.

We jumped on board with Captain Steve and his dog Boo. As we pulled away from the dock, he played the theme song from Gilligan's Island and was completely impressed when he discovered I knew every word. Captain Steve shared his knowledge of lobster fishing and granite excavation. He told stories of feuding fishermen and the rules of the sea. He found some seals for us, as promised, and then, as we were heading back to the shore, he posed the question that changed the course of our exploration:

"Would you like me to drop you off on a deserted island? I could pick you up in about an hour, at the end of my next tour."

I laughed, convinced he was joking. He asked three more times, challenging us that this may be our only opportunity to be completely alone on an island. Now, to me, this sounded like a familiar horror movie plot. You know, when you're watching the character make a really dumb choice and you're thinking, "Why would anyone do that?" And yet, in a matter of minutes, I was climbing a wooden ladder up a cliff and watching the boat sail away. As he drove off, he asked if we'd ever seen the movie *Deliverance,* and laughed (I am not making this up). Captain Steve mentioned there was a trail to our left, but we found nothing. We decided to explore Captain Steve's other left and went right where we came upon a path that took us deep into the woods. We were awestruck. Complete and utter silence. The ground was covered in all sorts of different mosses and felt soft and spongy beneath our feet. The air smelled of pine and salt. Every turn we took brought more beauty. When was the last time a human stood here? I felt like I was inside a terrarium. I also had a little voice inside my head that was suggesting Captain Steve may never return and I would live out my days here. I was suddenly glad I wasted all that time watching *Naked and Afraid.* I knew we would need to build a shelter and find a source of fresh water. I began scoping for berries.

We continued to follow the path, discovering a pond (fresh water source check) and some wildflowers. My mind kept going back to the fact that we were COMPLETELY ALONE...no one but Captain Steve knew where we were. I attempted to go live on Facebook, only to deplete my battery—the horror plot thickens. There was a constant battle in my head: beauty vs. fear. Next we stumbled across a quarry filled with water. Captain Steve told us that they had mined the granite many years ago. The path continued until we found ourselves in an open field, equally as beautiful with the tall grass blowing in the sea breeze, feeling the sun on our face, seeing the sign...wait...A SIGN? I thought this was a *deserted island...where man had not set foot in decades, maybe centuries!*

Sure enough, it was a parks and recreation sign telling us to leave the area as we had found it, blah, blah, blah. Okay, so maybe no one else was on the island, but we were far from being in unexplored territory (perhaps the ladder and the path should have been our first clue). We had a good laugh. We plopped on a rock, pulled out our survival trail mix, and waited for Captain Steve's return. And he did return, as promised.

The next day we headed to Acadia National Park for a day of hiking. We then headed back to Portland, spending a few hours in Bangor along the way. We had a fabulous last meal at *Duckfat*—a very trendy restaurant not to be missed if you are ever in Portland.

As I recall our adventure, I think about the times in my life when I've stepped out of my circle of ordinary. There have been times when God brought me into circumstances that I have never experienced before. I found myself fearful, yet hopeful, wanting desperately to trust God. I can easily testify that He has always been faithful. Keith and I thought we were in uncharted territory on that deserted island, in the precipice of danger, treading where no man had been in decades, only to find that the path we followed was previously laid for our discovery and pleasure.

...and, I'm pretty sure God giggled.

"I will never leave you, I will never abandon you."
Hebrews 13:5

Everyday Lessons

20

The Plant

was blessed to be able to move into a new home shortly after I was married. However, we had very little in the way of furnishings and decorations, and I was anxious to make it my *home.* After looking at hundreds of magazine photos, I decided that the one piece that could make a difference in my humble home was a big plant. Since I don't have much of a green thumb, I began my search for an inexpensive silk plant.

I found one in my budget (I think it was $9.95). It was a good size plant, a bit of a strange green, but doable. I was VERY proud of the addition to my living room. It was the perfect touch!

Years later we finished the lower level of our home, and now, since we had a "family," we added a family room. Again, not a lot of extra money for décor, but I had accumulated a few more things in my living room, so I was willing to sacrifice my plant and move it to the family room. It was the perfect touch!

Several years passed, and we decided to move to Oklahoma for some mission work. We found ourselves in a small apartment—the plant was delegated to the corner of the dining room. It was the perfect touch.

It wasn't long before I was given a cubicle in the office where I could have access to a computer. It was MY space, and it needed some love, so I placed the plant in the corner...the perfect touch.

The plant continued to follow me to my office at the church, then to my new home when we moved to Grove where it landed in the bathroom, and then to another new home where it spent some time in my daughter's bedroom. Later on down the road, I was given an office at The insurance agency where I worked. Of course, the plant was strategically placed in the corner.

It was at that time the plant succumbed to some criticism. It was now at least 14 years old, and it perhaps had faded a bit. Some of my coworkers shook their heads, but I was loyal to my plant.

When we moved our offices to a new building, I did some major decorating and purchased a new plant. I found a new place for the old plant in the office bathroom for a time (feeling rather proud of my generosity) before my employer replaced it with another new plant. It was then I found my dear friend placed at the back door, to go out with the garbage. I offered the plant to my coworkers for their office but all refused.

Are you kidding me? I rescued the plant and placed it in the attic, stating I might need it for a stage prop at some point. I was and am still serving as the drama director at our church.

Sure thing, years later, the Children's Christmas Program took place in a "park," so lots of greenery was needed. I hauled the plant to the church. It enjoyed being on stage—I could tell…it was the perfect touch. I felt like a proud momma. I decided to leave it in the storage room at church. Surely we would use it again at some juncture.

A week later I entered the sanctuary, ready to worship. The Christmas decorations were removed, and the church platform was returned to its normal status, except for one thing:

To this day, I still do not know who did it, but someone placed the plant next to the church piano, and the pianist was using it to camouflage her light. And there it stays…a very ordinary, well-used, somewhat faded plant, in a very prestigious place.

The only plant on our worship platform, I might add—and it's the perfect touch!

We are like my plant. God may move us around a lot, but everyplace He puts us is the perfect place. It may not be the most prestigious place, it may be as humble as a bathroom… but it's where we can best serve our purpose for that particular time. The world may ridicule or make us feel that we are not worth much, but our Heavenly Father knows where we've been and what we're capable of. He may even store us away for a time. We have no idea what is in store for us in the future. Where will we be placed next? How will God use us? That's the exhilaration of faith, of hope. We don't know, but we can trust.

Perhaps someday, we too may find a place we never expected to be, serving our God in a brand new way—FAR OUTSIDE OF ORDINARY!

Be kind to the plants.

21

Don't Miss the Party

When my brother Peter opened his law office, he hired me as his "Legal Secretary." I use the term lightly since I was only 18 and my training consisted of two semesters of high school typing. We were both rookies setting out on an adventure of faith and, no doubt, much more faith on his part. There's a treasure chest full of lessons learned during those years, but the first that comes to mind is "The Surprise Party."

Peter was turning thirty. To an 18-year-old that seemed like a huge milestone, and I thought it should be acknowledged in a big way. I took on the challenge of throwing him a surprise party. I called all the attorneys in town that I had ever spoken to or knew had with worked with Peter. I told them of his upcoming birthday, never considering the fact that it might not be as important to them as it was to me. I mean, "Come on," my oldest brother is turning thirty!"

Our office was situated next door to a popular fried chicken franchise, so it was easy to decide on the menu for the event. I ordered a cake from a favorite bakery and paid for it all out of my own pocket. This was a big feat for an 18-year-old. I giggled as I anticipated his surprise. My plan was to have some guests arrive before he returned from court that day and the remaining guests could filter in during their lunch hour. He was going to love this. What a great way for me to show him how much I loved him.

The day arrived. I picked up the cake on the way to work. I called the chicken restaurant and made sure they would have the food ready at just the right time so it would be warm. I laid out the plates and napkins and made sure the beverages were in place. I ran as fast as I could to the restaurant so I wouldn't miss the first guest. There—all set—and I waited. The chicken smelled so good! I worried about it getting cold. I waited and waited until...Peter walked through the door. His first question was: "Why does it smell like chicken in here?"

Surprise? I then had to explain to him that this was his surprise birthday party but no one showed up. Fortunately, he found it hilarious.

After a good laugh and a great big thank you, he went next door to my dad's tavern and invited all the regulars over for lunch. They came and enjoyed the meal and the cake and were happy to celebrate Peter's 30th birthday. Peter's attorney friend Jack did show up later. Peter is 64 now, and he and Jack went camping this year. REAL FRIENDS SHOW UP—EVEN FOR THE SILLY STUFF.

Does this story sound familiar? Matthew 22:1-14 tells the story of a King who sent out invitations to a wedding but all the guests had excuses why they couldn't attend. They were too busy or too distracted. Maybe they thought the event was insignificant and couldn't be bothered. Some were even malicious and killed the servants who brought the invitation. The King burned their city, and a new invitation was sent out. This time he sent his servants out to gather all who would attend: the good, the bad, it didn't matter. The King wanted to celebrate.

God invites you to the best party around. He invites you to worship him. Are you too distracted to attend?

The party's on...hope to see you there!

22

Face to Face

*J*oel is in the Army National Guard and has had the privilege of serving two deployments in Afghanistan. Those
were anxiety filled years for me. No words can describe how
much I missed him. The day of his first departure was traumatic
for me. I watched my son walk out the same door he used to go
to school, to go out to play, to go to work, to go to prom—but
this time he was in uniform with a pack on his back. He was going
to war. PLEASE GOD, BRING HIM HOME TO ME.

He drove off with his father, and I watched the car until I
could no longer see it. I folded under the weight of losing my
son that day. I wasn't the brave mother I wanted to be. I hurt so
bad my doctor medicated me and I went to bed. I woke to my
friend, Ivy placing a bracelet on my wrist. It had a star charm on
it that read:

"Hope, the feeling that what is wanted can be had."

I made the decision the bracelet would remain on my wrist until Joel returned to me safely. It reminded me every day that I would again see him face to face.

All of this happened years ago, before FaceTime and Skype. Webcams were the newest technology, and Joel suggested I get one so just maybe, if the timing was right, we could connect. Our internet connection was weak at best, so it was a long shot. We had several failed attempts, but one day Keith was online, just starting to shut down, and I heard the familiar "knocking" sound of the instant message. It meant that Joel had just come online. I screamed for Keith to stop; then I explained what the noise meant.

In a matter of a few seconds I was sent an invitation to see Joel on the webcam. It was finally going to happen! I pushed the accept button as fast as I could. The screen began to load, and my eyes filled with tears. I cried out, "Keith we're about to see our boy!"

And there he was! Words cannot express the joy of seeing his face. It really wasn't even that clear. He moved like a robot, and it would freeze up occasionally, but it was beautiful to me.

I thought about this later, and I was reminded of the scripture:

> *"Now all we can see of God is like a cloudy picture in a mirror. Later we will see him face to face. We don't know everything, but then we will."*
>
> *I Corinthians 13:12*

Our perception of Jesus is much the same. Through the Word of God, we have a glimpse of His beauty. When we pray and enter into praise, we can feel His presence. We can't see or understand clearly, but we know He is there. What we can comprehend is awesome. In the meantime we cling to what we know is true to give us a hope everlasting. We have the symbols of the cross, the communion bread and wine; the beautiful statues, paintings, and stained glass windows that remind of us of what Jesus did for us—much like how my bracelet reminded me of Joel. A day will come when we will no longer need the symbols. We will stand before our Savior and partake fully of His presence. We will see Him face to face.

The day Joel returned was by far the happiest day in my life. To see him march into the arena and, OH GLORY BE! When he saw our goofy sign and our eyes met for the first time...and then I got to hold my boy in my arms—joy unspeakable!

When we arrived home, I showed him the bracelet, and he took it off of my wrist. It was all behind us. I had never experienced such a joyous day, and yet I know it is only a fraction of the joy that will come when I see my Savior face to face. I will see Him. I will hug Him. The chains of this life will be removed, and I will be free for all eternity.

23

Trick or Treat

$\mathcal{H}$alloween fell on a Friday night, also known as date night. Keith and I decided to stay home in case we were blessed with children trick or treating (a rare event), and I opted to make a special dinner for us. I love to cook, and one of my favorite methods is to grab what's available in my kitchen and create something marvelous. With that said, I had noticed a package of meat in the freezer some time ago and wasn't exactly sure what it was...beef? Pork? We often buy meat in bulk and then package portions for two. All I knew is that there were two pieces of something and it was time to eat the mystery meat.

I grabbed my special spices and some vegetables from the fridge, and I was off. I sautéed some onions and mushrooms, added some zucchini and a little carrot for color. I generously seasoned my meat and let everything simmer. I added a touch of my favorite olive oil and some shaved Parmesan cheese, threw a yeast roll on the plate, and it looked and smelled terrific.

My husband "oohed" and "aahed." We thanked God for our food and dug in. And then it came:

"Hmmph."

"What's the matter?" I asked.

"Well, there's not very much meat...it's like all bone," he replied.

"Okay, so it's not the greatest piece of meat, but seriously, you put too much emphasis on meat. Concentrate on these marvelous vegetables. You have plenty to eat."

"Hmmph...but this is ridiculous. What kind of meat is this supposed to be?"

"REALLY? I don't know, beef or pork, who cares?" I then did my best to show him that there was sufficient meat on this bony steak until...well then, I said, "Does the meat taste a little funky?"

"Yes, it does. Where did you get it?"

"It was that little package that's been sitting in the freezer for a while." And then I had the revelation.

Last summer we grilled a couple of pork steaks, and instead of throwing the bones in the garbage, my husband suggested we wrap them and put them in the freezer to avoid excessively smelly garbage. He said he would grab them when he took the trash to the dump later in the week. He forgot.

So there you have it. I seasoned that trash, I sautéed that trash, I made that trash smell amazing. I even dressed that trash to the point we couldn't WAIT to dig in, but it was still trash...and I was sick the entire next day.

Is it just me, or does this remind you of sin? We look at it, we dress it up, and we make it look good. We convince ourselves that it can't be THAT bad. But it's still sin and it still makes us sick. How often do we postpone "throwing the sin out?" Instead, we put it away, out of sight. We may even forget about it for a while, but it shows up just when we think we have it all under control, and it makes us sick.

"Therefore, since we are surrounded by such a great cloud of witnesses, let us throw off everything that hinders and the sin that so easily entangles. And let us run with perseverance the race marked out for us." Hebrews 1:21 NIV

Then we won't have to wonder:
"Trick, or treat?"

24

Renovation

"Let us run with patience the race that is set before us, looking unto Jesus, the author and finisher of our faith." Hebrews 12:2

My son, Joel, bought his first house. It's a big house that needs lots of love and attention. Hero Husband and I headed his way recently to pitch in, along with my sister, and start spreading some love.

We were quite the renovation team. My sister, who had already been there for a week, took the lead with her list, assigning the prioritized jobs. It soon became evident who was good at what.

Hero Husband can fix just about **anything,** so he was the key player: laying floor, electrical issues, toilet issues, sticky door issues, move the heavy furniture – he was THE MAN;

Joel was a great assistant to THE MAN, but also had the brawn to pull up the nasty carpet that was insanely glued to the floor;

Sister Cindy was the visionary – she knew what needed to be done and how to get there. She's not afraid of hard work, in fact she covets the tough jobs, and she's pretty darn handy.

Me – well, initially it looked like I wasn't a very valuable asset. I'm not handy, I'm not strong, and I'm fairly clumsy. BUT...I love to **FINISH** things. I'm your girl for cleaning up the renovation messes. I'm your girl for the detail cleaning. I'm your girl to make the room feel "like home". So I tried my best to do my thing while everyone else seemed to be doing the important jobs. There was one point in our efforts that I knew I frustrated Cindy. Remember, she's looking at the big picture and all that needs to be done. She comes through the living room to find me vacuuming a pillow, (It truly needed vacuuming). The look on her face said it all: "We have bigger issues here than dirty pillows, really?" – but you know what? She held her tongue. I literally saw her take a breath and walk away – because she knew I was doing, well...what I do.

When renovating, different areas need different touches. And people have different renovating needs as well. Some of us need some deep repairs, others - a little tweaking, and still others, just some finishing touches. I've also noticed that I need different touches at different times. All that to say that I rejoice in knowing that Jesus is the author (He makes that priority list) and the FINISHER (have I mentioned how much I love finishing?) of our faith. He is taking our rough and ragged souls, and perfecting them over time as we continually submit our weaknesses to Him.

The super-duper important note here is that He **FINISHES,** and that provides hope for each and every one of us, no matter our current condition.

> **Whether you need a new foundation or just some accent touches – God is the ultimate and perfect renovator. Some jobs take a little longer than others, but He always finishes what He starts. He is happy to provide references upon request.**

25

Someone Needs to Knock

"Ask, and you will receive. Search, and you will find. Knock, and the door will be opened for you. Everyone who asks will receive. Everyone who searches will find. And the door will be opened for everyone who knocks."

Matthew 7:7-8

I was running late to class when I noticed the cute little coffee drive-thru. There was no way I had time, and I so needed a cup of coffee. Keep driving. The practical me reminded the passionate me that there would be coffee available at the class and probably some lovely pastries. "Dear Lord, please give me the strength to walk away from the pastries."

I arrived just in time and headed to the refreshment table. No pastries (prayer answered) and no coffee. What? Just soda and water. I don't drink soda. I need caffeine. I wanted coffee. I headed to the registration desk, completed my paperwork, and looking as pathetic as I could muster, I asked, "Is there ANYWHERE in this building where I could get a cup of coffee?"

The woman was so sweet (or maybe scared). She told me to have a seat and she would see if she could find some. Exhale. I was surprised and a little embarrassed when she came back with a coffee condiment tray and set it on the refreshment table. A few minutes later she reappeared with a large coffee dispenser and cups and then asked me how I would like my coffee. Oh my, I just wanted to steal a cup out of some secretary's Mr. Coffee, and it appears this woman is moving heaven and earth to satisfy my pathetic plea. My sister, Cindy always said I had whining down to a fine art.

"Black, just black."

I noticed some of the attendees glancing at me. I imagined they thought I was an annoying spoiled brat. "Sorry." She served me a large cup of piping hot Joe, and I was content. What happened next made me smile.

One by one, people left their seats to grab THEIR morning Joe. And even though no one thanked me, I knew they were grateful that I was brave enough and passionate enough to ask for that which I longed. YOU'RE WELCOME.

> **You don't always know what's on the other side of the door when you knock. It may be a simple cup of coffee, or it may be an opportunity to make the world a better place.**

26

The Perfect Imperfection

One of my dearest friends is at that difficult stage in life where her mother is failing physically and mentally. Her family recently moved her mother into a nursing home, which gave my friend the opportunity to sort through her mother's belongings and take what she might like to keep. As she was sorting through some items in her mother's buffet, she found a very unique tea set that she hadn't seen in years. She immediately remembered where her mother had the set displayed when she was a child, and my friend was so excited to have the opportunity to bring it into her own home. She carefully wrapped the teapot, sugar bowl, and creamer in paper to prepare it for her journey home.

She thought about the tea set as she drove, recalling that it had been in the family a long time. She thought it may have once belonged to her aunt, but its origin was that it was a gift from her grandfather to his mother. Needless to say, it was a treasure.

When she arrived home, she carefully removed the set from the box and unwrapped the tissue paper. She filled her sink with warm, soapy water, and gently placed the fragile pieces in the water. She noticed that some of the gold had worn off, and her imagination took her to a different era, where perhaps the delicate pot was used to entertain guests on Sunday afternoons in the parlor. The ladies were in beautiful dresses, enjoying a cup of tea with their biscuits, engaged in amusing conversation with their friends, while the gentlemen were on the porch discussing their latest business pursuits.

She gently washed the sugar bowl, and as she ran her fingers along the porcelain, her finger came upon an unexpected ridge. She lifted the bowl, turned it over, and gasped as she looked down upon the evidence of a repaired crack. The memory immediately flooded her mind as she recalled an evening long ago. She and her brothers were home alone, and someone was roughhousing in the dining room. The sugar bowl was knocked off the table and broke upon impact. It didn't matter who knocked it, she was in charge of her brothers, and she would be blamed and punished for the incident. She was confident and fearful that the punishment would be severe, so she went into action. She located the Elmer's glue and commenced. She very carefully glued the broken piece and put it in place on the bowl. She held it tightly together, blew on it, and watched the glue dry. She then took a damp cloth and wiped the excess glue away. She then returned the sugar bowl to the top of the buffet. She stood and stared at it. She casually "walked by" the buffet to see if she could notice where it was broken. The next day she carefully picked it up and felt where it was broken to see if she could notice where it was repaired. She was happy with the results. Over the next year or so, she would pick up the sugar bowl and inspect it. Eventually she completely forgot the whole incident, until...

She finished drying the tea set and let it sit on the kitchen counter. What teenager would have ever thought that as Elmer's glue aged, it would yellow or turn a brownish color? She congratulated herself for her success at being able to keep her mother from a major meltdown and smiled knowing her brothers must have been thankful their sister took care of the accident. It has been over 40 years since it was broken, the actual age of the set is unknown, but it is definitely an heirloom. My friend was offered an opportunity to get the yellowed crack professionally repaired in order to add to its value, but she opted to let it stay. To her, it adds another generation's story, and that value is priceless.

I love this story because it reminds me that emotional and physical scars always tell a story. It's what we do with those stories that determine the value of the occurrence. I have suffered a fair share of trauma in my life, and yet I am confident that I would not be who I am today, or who I will become tomorrow, had I not walked through those dark times. Not all wounds just vanish, but the memories that remain build our character and enable us to be more loving and compassionate with others. This is a significant step outside our circle of expectation. The scars you bear add to your story, your value...and you, my friend, are priceless in His sight.

> *"I am sure what we are suffering now cannot compare with the glory that will be shown us."*
>
> *Romans 8:18*

27

Look Who Came to Dinner

*"While Jesus was having dinner at Matthew's house,
many tax collectors and sinners came and ate with
him and his disciples."*

Matthew 9:10 NIV

*I*t happened on Easter Sunday. I was sitting at church and started thinking: Jesus was known for eating with those who the Pharisees, the "spiritual leaders" of the day, considered undesirable. Tax collectors (those particularly known for scamming others), prostitutes, the unemployed and the sick were welcomed at his table. And there I was on Easter Sunday, preparing to take communion in a room full of people. We were invited to eat at the table with Jesus. Look who came to dinner! What would the Pharisees say if they were to observe THIS dinner party?

Let's take inventory of who is in the room. Now I don't know who is who, but I can pretty much bet there are some with a fairly dark past...or maybe even present...they don't feel like they really belong here—simply not worthy. There are probably a few people here who are looking across the room and thinking "Yeah, YOU need to be in church, buddy. I know who you are outside of these walls —maybe God will get a hold of you today." Then there are most likely one or two sitting here because the person next to them guilted them into being here, and they just wish they could get home to their ham dinner and chocolate bunny. Some are here because, well, they're always here. It's what you do on Sunday... blah, blah, blah. I could go on and on.

The bottom line is that if the Pharisees were standing in the room, they would be pointing fingers and feeling pretty good about themselves. But fortunately for us, it's not about the Pharisees. It's about Jesus and how He looks in our hearts and sees the beauty of His creation. He invites US to dine with Him. He invites US to remember how He died so we can be forgiven and begin anew. He invites US to know He lives today, continually pouring out His grace and His mercy so we can walk in righteousness. It's the very reason we celebrate not only on Easter but every Sunday morning and every single day.

My brother Frankie likes to quote a line from the movie *Cool Hand Luke*: "GET YOUR MIND RIGHT." That's my challenge for you today. Put aside all the judgments, shame, boredom, selfishness, and preconceived ideas for a few minutes and have dinner with Jesus. Close your eyes and thank Him. Maybe reintroduce your-self to Him. Spend a few moments and celebrate His life. You don't have to be in church to experience His presence.

He's available to catch a bite on the fly.

28

Who Doesn't Love a Good Mall?

"You will seek me and find me when you seek me with all your heart. I will be found by you."

Jeremiah 29:13 NIV

I love to shop. No, I mean I am PASSIONATE about shopping. Every few weeks I just have to look for something special, and I am tenacious. I love the thrill of finding a good deal or finding the perfect something I've long been looking for. Oh the joy of finding something wonderful you weren't even looking for! My blood is rushing as I type.

I'm not sure what initiated my shopping passion. My mother wasn't a shopper. Maybe I can blame Cindy. One thing for sure, I passed the torch to Grace. For Grace's third birthday, we had our first "Girls' Day Out." We went to the mall, she got her first real haircut, I let her pick out a new outfit, and we topped the day off with getting her ears pierced. And yes, for those of you judging me right now, it's true I created a bit of a monster. However, Grace went on to graduate from the Fashion Institute of Technology and now has a successful career in the fashion industry...AND she buys her mother clothes from time to time. So there.

There are all sorts of "shoppers." There are those who NEED something specific and go to the store and buy the first thing they find that could possibly fulfill the need. They are boring and reckless. There are those who hate wasting time at the mall so they do the majority of their shopping online. This can be exhilarating but lacks physicality (not to mention the Godiva chocolates and/or cupcake breaks). There are those who shop because they enjoy new and pretty things, but they don't really have fun with the process. These people just need guidance and maybe a little training. Then... there's Grace and me:

> *Let's get this day rolling and head to the mall as soon as we can get out the door...woohoo!!!!!!!!*

We are willing to travel for hours if the mall is worthy of the perfect hunt. We will spend the ENTIRE day going from store to store looking for special sale items or unique pieces. We will try on LOTS of clothes "just to see what they might look like." Sometimes we try on the same thing just to compare. She's a size 0 so she almost always wins that game...but that's okay. After all, I made her. The day will include a delightful lunch, a coffee, and perhaps a cupcake or truffle. We will have to make as least one extra trip to the car to unload. When we get home, we have a "Treasure Bath" and review all of our fabulous finds.

So where am I headed with all this hedonism? Yes, friend, I AM aware of my lack of spirituality thus far. The thought occurred to me the other day—of where would I be if I approached my spiritual life like I approach shopping? Let's rewrite that last paragraph a bit.

I spend the entire day going from my Bible, to listening to Christian music, to Christian fellowship—looking for wisdom, knowledge, discernment and encouragement. I will read LOTS of scripture "just to find a new revelation." Sometimes I try on a new attitude or God changes my perspective. The day includes spiritual nourishment, a worship song to pick me up, and maybe even an unexpected blessing. The day will include at least one conversation with a friend...just to share the joy of the day. And when the day is through...I will bask in the gratitude of God's grace.

Get the picture? What are you passionate about? Consider the energy you put toward your passion, the process and the satisfaction you gain.

Passion brings tenacity, and that tenacity will produce tremendous treasure.

Lord, I want to be passionate and tenacious in my walk with you. I not only want to discover your many treasures, but I want to share them with others...and Lord, by the way, thank you for the joy of shopping with my daughter.

29

Not My Ordinary Breakfast

*I*t was Wednesday, and on Wednesday morning I usually make myself a protein shake for breakfast. I always make a little extra for my hubby to help keep him fit and give him a little boost in his day. On this particular Wednesday I was especially motivated to make my shake as energy packed as possible because I was sending Keith off to Royal Family Kids Camp. He serves as a counselor at this terrific camp for foster kids.

I combined my usual unsweetened vanilla almond milk, protein powder, and chia seeds. To ramp up this shake, I added a banana and my special, energy-packed surprise...the remainder of the moringa leaves I had in the freezer. I purchased these at a Farmer's Market, and they are vitamin packed. Now they were in the freezer for a bit, so they were covered with ice crystals. "Hmmm, I wonder if they're still good?"

I convinced myself they were just fine and that the ice crystals would just help chill the drink. Since there wasn't much in the package, I just dumped in all the contents and pushed the start button on my blender. I poured my yummy beverage into my tall glass, added a straw, and then poured some into Keith's small glass, no straw. We were set.

I sat down in my morning chair, grabbed my iPad, turned to my devotion, and took a nice long draw on my straw. Whoa... what is this weird sensation in my mouth? Tingle?—NO, more like burning! Was there something wrong with mixing moringa leaves with a banana...no wait...I recognize this taste! Oh, no, those weren't the moringa leaves, I poured in the package of diced jalapenos!!! My throat and my stomach were on fire. Now, let me tell you THAT was a "step out of my circle of expectation!"

Keith comes to see what all the commotion is about, and I proclaim "DO NOT DRINK THAT SHAKE!" I quickly explain what I had done, and what does he do? He takes a sip! He knows what's in it, and he still TAKES A SIP! He shouts "GOOD GRIEF THAT'S AWFUL!"

"Ya think? I warned you!" Call me crazy, but Adam and Eve flashed thru my mind.

Life, our own conscience, and most importantly, the Word of God, present us with all sorts of warnings. We're all guilty of ignoring them from time to time.

Warnings have merit. An element of danger always precedes a warning—something happened to someone, somewhere that caused someone to say "be careful here." It only makes sense that we would be wise to heed them. It could save us from a lot of unnecessary "burning".

30

From the Mouths of Babes

I was attending a Sunday morning service in Long Island City, New York. At the time, it was a small church, meeting in a borrowed restaurant. I was sitting behind a young couple with an infant. I am not what you would call a "baby person," but being grandchild deprived, I was a bit distracted and mesmerized by this little human. The mother seemed comfortable holding the baby as she swayed to the worship songs. The baby was content at first, but as I watched, I noticed his little face showing twitches of discomfort. The mother's eyes were closed, and she didn't notice that his innocence was fading fast. Or, maybe she did...because within moments the baby twisted, clenched his hands, whimpered, and the mother's hand swiftly reached into her bag, bringing a bottle to the baby's mouth before I could say, "Hey, your baby's about to bust and disrupt the service."

Now, this is the good part...for just a second or two the baby fought the intrusion of the bottle, but one taste of that comfort, and he was committed. With fists clenched and a scowl on his face, he went after it with aggression, and then something beautiful happened. His sucking slowed, his furrowed brow released, and his little fists ever so slowly opened. Right there before me was a perfect portrait of complete peace. His little mouth let go of the bottle and he slept.

I don't remember the sermon that day, but I remember the Holy Spirit speaking to my heart. Sometimes life is just plain hard. Circumstances weigh heavily. It's easy to feel sorry for myself, overwhelmed, wrought, confused, angry...filled with frustration. But when I choose to fill my mind, soul and spirit with the Word of God, it isn't long before my fists unclench and I find peace.

"Be like newborn babies who are thirsty for the pure spiritual milk that will help you grow and be saved."
I Peter 2:2

31

What I Learned from Barbie

I spent a lot of time playing by myself as a child. Many of my weekends were spent at my Grandmother's house. Now, Grandma taught me how to cook, how to clean, play cards, Yahtzee, Dominoes, and she exposed me to the arts via The Lawrence Welk Show. She secretly had a penchant for soap operas, The Brady Bunch, and Planet of the Apes movies, so there's that.

On a typical Saturday after morning cartoons, I would play with my Barbie dolls in the living room while Grandma sat in her rocking chair. Today I would like to invite you into my Barbie community because, as I reminisce about my playtime, I realize how much my life reflects those early days of imagination. To be honest, I think Barbie should get some credit in my upbringing.

Let me start with some introductions. My Barbie family actually started with some hand-me-down "Tammy" dolls. There was, of course, Tammy, who was a bit stockier than Barbie, and had a weird shoot of long hair in the center of her head. There were Tammy's parents, who I affectionately named Frank and Dorothy after my own parents. Tammy had three younger siblings, Wendy, probably about 15 years old (because she never drove). There was Pepper who, in my mind, struggled with her weight and had bad red hair—maybe 13, and her little brother Salty, maybe 8. Now, there was also Bob, who sometimes was Tammy's older brother and sometimes her boyfriend. (Hey, the population was limited, so think Biblical times, and this won't seem so scandalous). As time progressed, I added these Barbies: There was Midge, who was strong-willed, smart, but not quite as pretty as her blonde sister/friend, Francine, who had a collection of hair pieces. There was, of course, Barbie, who had it all. OH, and there was Misty, who had really bad hair (older doll that had white hair that you were supposed to be able to color with special markers (but it didn't take long for that to go south). Midge, Francine, and Barbie were always trying to help Misty look better because she often played the role of the cousin whose parents died so she had to come live with this family of cousins. And of course, there was Ken, who all the girls fought over (poor Bob was always second choice). Now you've met the cast of characters.

Almost every Saturday I would pull out my cases and boxes of dolls and clothes and set up the house on the small, oval rug in front of Grandma's gray plaid sofa. The sofa became the second story of the house. I kept a lot of the clothes in an old wooden silverware box that I always placed on the right. It served as a dining room table, a dance floor (when we threw the ball), and the stage (when we had the talent shows). Frank and Dorothy always slept in the plaid case downstairs. Wendy, Pepper, and Salty's rooms were in the east wing on the main floor, and the older girls slept upstairs. Once again, Bob sometimes stayed in the house (on top of the back of the couch aka "the attic"), but Ken only visited, unless he was sleeping over, in which case he would stay in the aforementioned attic. One more important caveat: Since I only had a blue plastic boat for transportation, the family lived on an island, and my Grandmother's carpet was now the sea. There were harbors available underneath any chair in the room, but you had to be VERY careful around the rocking chair lest you get crushed.

I can genuinely say that the many hours in this world of imagination played a key role in the adult I became. Go ahead and laugh, but consider these facts: I think I always saw myself as "Tammy," a little overweight, a little weird, and never fully accepted by the pretty girls. Yet Tammy always overcame the obstacles at the end of the day and got to wear the prettiest dress (handmade by Grandma, because the Barbie dresses were always too tight). Please note that Tammy was always the one who helped Cousin Misty (the one with the bad hair) by being accepting of her and finding her the perfect outfit.

Oh yes, let's talk about the clothes. The Barbie family was ALWAYS changing clothes. I was fortunate enough to have quite a collection along with accessories. Now, in real life, I love clothes; my closet is like a giant silverware box. I have outfits for every occasion, and again, note I loved dressing up my own daughter Grace so much that she went on to graduate from the Fashion Institute of Technology.

Okay, moving on. If the Barbie family wasn't having a formal ball where EVERYONE, except Salty, got dressed to the hilt (Salty only had one outfit so he always had to go to bed early), then they were putting on a talent show (Salty was welcomed at this event). The talent show was a huge endeavor because I had to create an act (not to mention costumes) for all the participants. This is where I learned my production skills. Reality check—as an adult I worked as a dance instructor, wedding coordinator, drama teacher, and I am still active in our Community Theater as an actress and director. Since I absolutely love throwing a good party, I think the balls played a major part in my hospitality skills, and to this day, I enjoy spending hours getting ready for an event.

I learned a lot about important things like relational conflicts as Midge, Tammy, Francine, and Misty tried to get along with Barbie. There was always a lot of apologizing after afternoons of conflict. I learned that even though Ken rarely looked Tammy's way, Bob was actually the better guy. After all, Bob was always the clown in the talent show because Ken's legs were too rubbery to get into the clown costume. Who doesn't love the "funny" guy? And, even though Bob couldn't bend his legs, who wants a guy with rubber legs?

I learned a lot about adventure, as the Barbie family loved to strike out on the boat...sometimes on transcontinental excursions to Grandma's bedroom. There were romantic dates, picnics, and shipwrecks. There may be danger lurking, but you could always count on another family member to save you in the plaid dingy (aka Frank and Dorothy's bedroom). FAMILY IS ALWAYS THERE IN THE ROUGH TIMES.

What I most want to thank the Barbie family for is the gift of imagination they so generously gave me. They helped me through some lonely days, and they were faithful to teach me an incredible life lesson:

> *It always works out in the end...as long as you keep playing.*

A couple of questions that creep me out a little: when I was caught up in all of my Barbie world drama, did I talk out loud, or was it all in my head? Did Grandma sit in her rocking chair and listen to all of this every weekend? Hmmmm...maybe that's why she loved having me stay with her. There were no soap operas on Saturdays.

32

Garden Space

I love flowers. I fell in love with them when I was a little girl. I was fascinated by daisies, daffodils, tulips, you name it. Mrs. Cadarian, my neighbor, had tulips in her yard, and I thought they were the most magical flower ever. I longed to grow beautiful flowers of my own, so I asked my Mom if I could have a garden. I offered to buy the seeds and do everything myself. Her initial reply was, "It's hard to grow flowers," and she did her best to discourage me. The real truth was that she didn't share the same fascination as I did, and she had no experience with gardening. I was a pretty determined child, so I began to scout out the perfect location for my garden. I soon noticed the lack of landscaping on the east side of our house, and I quickly inquired if I could plant some flowers there, under my bedroom window.

Again she told me the ground would be hard and rocky, and I would have a difficult time, but she gave me the go-ahead to try. She also instructed me to remove all the grass and weeds before planting the seeds.

I bought a packet of Cosmos seeds and found a small garden spade. Now, if you've ever tried to dig with a garden spade in hard, dry, rocky soil, then you know this was a tough endeavor for a little girl. I tried to pull the grass and weeds out of my 4 x 3 plot, but I left most of the roots behind. It wasn't long before I was discouraged and considered that maybe my mom was right—maybe gardening was too hard.

I told my Dad of my struggle, and he came to investigate. He walked away, and in minutes returned with a big spade. I watched as my Dad dug deep and overturned the dirt. I watched him pluck the weeds and grass and dig some more. He found a few rocks and pitched those aside. I remember feeling bad because my Dad seemed to be working so hard—but at the same time, I was amazed at his strength and how what seemed impossible for me, was fairly easy for him. It really only took a few minutes, and I had my first garden plot. My dad left me with my seeds, reminding me to be careful to follow the planting directions and to keep the seeds wet.

I anxiously planted my seeds in careful rows and watered them every day. It seemed to take forever, but when I saw the first hint of green, I leaped with excitement. I was growing my own flowers! What a joy it was to watch those little plants grow bigger every day, and soon they had little buds. I could hardly wait for them to bloom. It seemed to take the whole summer, but eventually my flowers bloomed and bloomed. It was breathtaking! I would visit them each day and just gaze at the flowers *I planted.* Part of me wanted to pick them, but then they would be gone, and my garden wouldn't be so pretty anymore. I decided to let them be.

Reflecting back on my first garden experience seems like a parable: I had a dream—people discouraged me. Undaunted, I moved forward, only to consider that when things got hard, maybe they were right. But rather than give up, I called out to my father for help. My father showed up and used a tool much bigger than what I had in my arsenal, and he moved the obstacles out of my way. He encouraged me to be careful to follow directions and warned me to be faithful in caring for my garden even before I could see any plants. I moved forward in obedience. There was a season of waiting, a glimpse of hope, but still more waiting. And then the glorious day came when the buds burst forth, the colorful flowers bloomed, and the desire of my heart was manifested. I had my own garden,

> *...and I couldn't have accomplished it without my father.*

But that's not the end of the garden story: One day the lady across the street (my friend's mom) had a heart attack. It was my first exposure to someone I knew having to be rushed to the hospital by ambulance. It was very scary for me, and I was worried about her. My friend asked me if I would go to the hospital with her to visit her mom. I remembered seeing on TV that when people are sick, you should bring them flowers. I looked long and hard at my flowers. This felt like a sacrifice, but it made me happy to use my beautiful flowers for such a noble cause.

I carefully cut my flowers and bundled them with a ribbon. I'm pretty sure Mrs. Redington didn't know the magnitude of my generosity, but she was indeed touched by my kindness, and you know what...I really liked the feeling of giving something that cost me something. I experienced *sacrifice,* and even as a child, it resounded as truth within my spirit. One of my favorite scriptures in the Bible is found in II Samuel 24:24:

> *"For I will not present burnt offerings to the Lord, my God, that have cost me nothing."*

There's certainly joy when we give out of our abundance, but it's a different story when it costs us something. It's the kind of joy that sets the Holy Spirit dancing within us.

> ***...and who doesn't love a good twirl around the floor?***

33

Heavenly Fruit

I rejoice because God can change the things that I am powerless to change. I've been thinking a lot about His transforming grace.

> *"God's Spirit makes us loving, happy, peaceful, patient, kind, good faithful, gentle, and self-controlled." Galatians 5:22*

When we apply any one of these "fruits" to a situation it transforms it into something beautiful. Apply love to anger and it produces forgiveness. Apply patience to aggravation and it produces grace. Apply gentleness to ignorance and it produces understanding. And the list goes on.

Love is a gift. Love is from God and love is because of God. God is love. Without God there is no love. Love is a gift.

"And so we know and rely on the love God has for
us. God is love. Whoever lives in love lives in God,
and God in them." I John 4:16 NIV

We cannot truly love outside of the love of God. We can feel warm feelings, passion, compassion, delight, but real love is a commitment. Real love can be tough. Mother Teresa said, "Don't look for big things, just do small things with great love... the smaller the thing, the greater must be our love."[1] It's in the seemingly insignificant acts or choices we make where real love is demonstrated. It's when we choose to live, not for our own gain, but to bring pleasure to our Creator. Love is a gift.

There's always joy.

"Rejoice in the Lord always, I will say it again:
Rejoice."

Philippians 4:4 NIV

I am working on joy. I'm simply thinking about it; I am looking for it (it's hard to find in some circumstances) and when all else fails, I'm REJOICING in the hope that "this too shall pass." I'm doing my best to bring joy to others with words of encouragement and sincere interaction. I'm finding joy in the simple things

---

[1] Mother Theresa, Come Be My Light, Brian Kolodiejehukk, M.C., ed (New York: Double day, 2007) 34

that bring me comfort...a cup of warm coffee, a belly laugh, or a kind word. Not only do I want to find JOY, I want to bring JOY. I believe with all my heart that God works in me, through me, and around me...I just need to open my heart.

Peace is a place. It's the shelter in the storm:

> *"Whoever dwells in the shelter of the Most High will rest in the shadow of the Almighty."*
>
> *Psalm 91:1 NIV*

It's the quiet in the chaos:

> *"Be still and know that I am God." Psalm 46:10 NIV*

It's the rest in the turmoil:

> *"The Lord will fight for you; you need only be still." Exodus 14:14 NIV*

It's the comfort of His arms:

> *"He tends his flock like a shepherd; He gathers the lambs in his arms and carries them close to His heart."Isaiah 40:11 NIV*

He is able to deliver you from any situation. Your circumstances may not change but your perspective will.

> *"Come to me all who are weary and heavy burdened and I will give you rest." Matthew 11:28 NIV*

Patience is a decision. It's your choice. Can you trust that, even in the midst of delays, frustrations, anger or disrespect that God still reigns? Could it be that the very thing the enemy is using to drive you "crazy" is actually God working in you:

> *"...To will and to act in order to fulfill his good purpose."*
> *Philippians 2:13 NIV*

Your choice: growl or grow. Kindness is an action. Why do we say people are kind? How do we know they are kind...because they *did something:*

> *"Be kind and compassionate to one another."*
> *Ephesians 4:32 NIV*

Get up, get going, and spread it like a virus! Goodness is obedience. Read the Bible and do what it says:

"If anyone, then, knows the good they ought to do it, and doesn't do it, it is sin for them." James 4:17 NIV

Faithfulness is determination. It's an attitude, it's a decision already made. Take a big bite...it will get you to the end.

"Therefore, since we are surrounded by such a great cloud of witnesses, let us throw off everything that hinders and the sin that so easily entangles. And let us run with perseverance the race marked out for us." Hebrews 12:1 NIV

Gentleness is humility. Gentleness doesn't see the sin. Gentleness doesn't feel the wrath. Gentleness comes from compassion, from understanding. Gentleness comes from knowing that love is needed.

"Be completely humble and gentle; be patient, bearing with one another in love." Ephesians 4:2 NIV

Self-control is a discipline. I always think of eating when I think of self-control. This is due to the fact that, when my mouth is full of food, I experience enormous pleasure...and an expanding waistline. Self-control is more like kale than fruit. It's a super-food that doesn't always taste so good. Self-control, like all the other fruits, starts with a choice and takes effort and practice. It almost always means denying yourself and choosing God's way. Without it, you're nothing short of a hot mess.

> *"Losing self-control leaves you as helpless as a city without a wall."*
>
> *Proverbs 25:28*

I have no idea where you are in your life right now, but I do know that God is there and He has everything you need in order to move forward. I pray that you lean on Him, look for ways to let Him work in you and through you—to produce the fruit that not only changes you but also changes the situations and people around you.

Eat until you are full!

34

Buzz Kill

"After the meal, he took another cup of wine in his hands. Then he said "this is my blood. It is poured out for you, and with it, God makes his new agreement. The one who will betray me is here at the table with me! The Son of Man will die in the way that has been decided for him, but it will be terrible for the one who betrays him!" Then the apostles started arguing about who would ever do such a thing. The apostles got into an argument about which one of them was the greatest." Luke 22:20-24

When reading this scripture most people focus on the communion aspect, but I am intrigued by what happens at the end. We find the disciples questioning each other as to who might betray Jesus and then arguing about who was the greatest. One of the most significant moments in history is right before them, but they are completely distracted by how and where they fit into the picture.

I giggled this morning when I read this because I immediately thought of those quizzes you find on the internet. The ones that help you figure out your true personality or who should play you in a movie or where you should actually live or...well, you get the picture. Too bad the disciples couldn't take a quiz to see who was most likely to betray Jesus or who was actually the greatest.

Keith makes fun of me for taking these quizzes. I can't help myself—I think they're fun. I have even more fun making him think that I believe they are highly scientific. He gets so frustrated (another giggle). Just the other day I was "proving" their authenticity when I explained to him that my latest test result declared that I had the same personality traits as Princess Diana, Oprah, and Gandhi. He just stared at me as if I was out of my mind, which offended me a little because, quite frankly, I think I see the similarities.

But we're off track here, which is what I wanted to point out about the scripture. Jesus is having one of the most life-changing moments during His time on earth, and the disciples are worried about who's going to do what and who's the greatest. How often do we see this in our own lives—whether we're at church, speaking with a friend, or just having a teachable moment in our lives, and we miss the significance of the moment because we're caught up in the cares of the world...like:

- Did I turn the crock pot down to low?
- What day is my doctor's appointment again?

- She really needs to touch up her roots!
- When are leggings appropriate?

My point is: Sometimes we get caught up in the "mysteries" of life when the truth is right in front of us. God is speaking to our hearts, and we miss it. When we turn our eyes to Jesus and open our hearts to Him, the whys and wherefores can be put aside. We can trust that the author and finisher of our faith will be a lamp unto our feet. When you spend time in communion with God, the rest falls into place. Don't miss out on what God wants to teach you today.

You can always check out the Buzz Feed quizzes...if you have an open mind, you can learn a lot. Okay, so maybe not really. I took one not long ago that concluded which of the 12 disciples I would have been. I'm pretty sure I must have misunderstood some questions.

I would have been Judas...seriously?

In the Name
of
Beauty

35

Sin Stinks

I confess, I am a beauty product addict. I continually promise myself that I will refrain from obtaining any new creams, lotions, elixirs, or makeup until I use what I have. But then a product will catch my eye, promising great improvement, and I can't resist trying it.

Not too long ago, I was browsing through a magazine when something caught my eye. It was a column from a beauty editor… you know, one of those people with the job of trying new beauty products and relaying the results to those of us who can only dream of a job like that. It was the title of her column, "The Best Beauty Advice I Ever Received," that grabbed me. That's a huge statement for someone who tries new products almost daily. This was huge! This would be a golden nugget of information.

She proceeded to pass on a home recipe passed down from her Grandmother, promising to give your hair the perfect shine. Grandma claimed that when you felt a little dull, you just needed to give your hair a good shine, and you would have a whole new outlook.

Well, I wasn't too motivated by the new outlook, but I would love to have shiny hair, so I gathered the ingredients, one of which was an egg yolk.

Now, here's where the story gets interesting. The directions were a bit vague:

Mix products / apply to hair / wrap hair in towel for 30 minutes / rinse.

Here's where I got perplexed...where does the shampoo come in? At the salon, the shine treatment comes after the shampoo, so I went with that theory. My hair was definitely slick and shiny after my rinse. And after it dried...well, it was still quite slick, rather reminiscent of the girl in grade school who rarely washed her hair. But the worst part was my hair smelled like an egg. I endured it for the night because I so desperately wanted to reap the full benefit of the shine treatment. I washed it first thing in the morning, and it really did look shiny. I mean, WOW, this was pretty amazing.

Then I stepped outside for just a minute whereupon the sun hit my hair and the humidity ran its fingers through my locks, giving off the scent of a rotten egg! Surely this was just my imagination playing a trick on me. So I rewashed it, adding conditioner, and headed off to work. Throughout the day, particularly when I stepped into the sun, my head radiated the essence of a hen house. I apologized to my coworkers, and they just rolled their eyes.

Sin is like that. We want the pleasure of something we don't have. We put the effort into making it happen. We enjoy the short-term results, but after a while, it starts to smell. And sometimes, even when we've been forgiven and washed in the blood, the people around us still get a whiff of the sin. It's why sometimes we feel we can't move forward in life—family, friends, society can still smell the fragrance of a past mistake. Maybe you've made a wrong choice, even though you know you've asked for forgiveness, every once in a while, the consequences of your sin show up and it stinks.

When Jesus sat down and broke bread with His disciples, He asked them to believe the blood that was about to be poured out was for the forgiveness of sin. Forgiveness takes faith. They didn't understand it then, and they certainly didn't understand it when they watched Him suffer on the cross. But they did understand it when they met the resurrected Christ, and so will you. Do you believe that the covenant laid out on that table that night was for you? Do you believe that God can take the dark corners of your life and use them for good? Do you believe that God forgives you even when others don't?

I encourage you today to walk in the faith of your forgiveness. God wants you to know how very much He loves you. So when the devil reminds you of where you have been, you just simply need to remind him where you are going. The world may still smell the stain of your sin, but God smells the blood of his one and only Son

...and there is no fragrance more pleasing to Him.

36

Pantyhose

here are lessons to be learned every day if you are willing to take a good look. Take pantyhose for instance. Yes, I said pantyhose. Keith refers to them as "sausage casings," which is probably a reflection on my legs, but I choose to not dwell on that thought. Pantyhose are one of those things that, as a child I couldn't wait to experience, and as an adult I wish I didn't need them—right along with eye glasses, makeup, hair color, and shaving my legs.

My first lesson was the first time Mom allowed me to wear pantyhose with my plaid school uniform. This meant trading in my knee-high socks and bruised knees for smooth, beautiful, "suntanned" legs. As I pulled on said suntan, I noticed a little "nub" and asked Mom if I should cut it off.

"NO," she said emphatically. "DO NOT PULL THAT, IT WILL RUIN YOUR HOSE."

I marched off to school with confidence and hoped all the other knee- high sock girls would be jealous of my new, sophisticated look. As the day wore on, I kept running my finger over that "nub" on my leg. I pulled it just a little, and nothing horrible happened. I don't know what possessed me, or why I had to find out—I just did. You guessed, it I pulled that nub and my hose split, causing a run all the way down my leg. My friends all had a good giggle. My Mom, however, did not giggle; and I realized, *maybe my Mom knows what she's talking about.*

My next lesson came in middle school, when I truly began to compare myself to the girls who were prettier, smarter, and much more liked. Try as I might, I never measured up, maybe because I continually had runs in my stockings. But there was one girl, who was not only beautiful, she (struggling to find a tactful way to say this), she...had a chest that was actually worthy of a bra. I was jealous, and it was obvious by the boys' stares that I wasn't the only one impressed by this phenomenon. So what does this have to do with pantyhose you ask? Well, do you remember "L'eggs" pantyhose—famous for their packaging in those white eggs that screwed apart? If not, ask your Mom. It just so happened that after a sleepover with some friends, it was disclosed that little Miss Dolly Parton was being enabled by strategically placed "L'eggs" eggs tops. *The pretty girls aren't always what they seem.*

My final lesson is the one that impacted my life the most. A few years after I became a Christian, Keith and I moved to a "mega" church. I began helping out with the youth a little, and eventually

I was asked to teach a high school Sunday school class. I agreed to the challenge, but I was really nervous. I did not know these teenagers, but I was well aware that teenagers could be tough. Most of the kids attended a Christian high school and probably knew more about the Bible than I did. I knew I would have to be REALLY interesting to engage a teenager at 9 o'clock on Sunday morning. I gave myself a good pep talk and prayed my guts out. Just before entering the first class, I went for one last bathroom break and a quick touch-up. (You only have one chance to make a first impression, and well, cuteness goes a long way) and one more prayer: "God, PLEASE give me favor with these kids, help me to be funny and to win them over."

The door was in the rear of the classroom. I peeked in and saw that the room was almost full of students sitting at their desks. I took a deep breath and walked in, down the center aisle. The room went completely silent, and then I heard a few giggles as I reached the podium. I noticed all eyes were on me. A little weird—even I know I'm not THAT cute. I introduced myself, and then a girl from the front row sheepishly stood up and approached me. She leaned in and whispered words I never want to hear again:

"Miss Lori, your dress is tucked inside your pantyhose."

"I'm sorry, what?"

"Here, let me help you," she said quietly as she gently pulled my dress from its captivity.*

"Thank you, and class, now that I have your attention, let's start our lesson on humility."

God enjoys a good belly laugh.

There is a beautiful jewel in this young lady's Heavenly crown as the result of this incident.

37

How Do You Smell?

*L*et's continue with our discussion on smell just a bit longer. Smelling good is a priority to most of us and, hopefully, it's important to the people you surround yourself with. I took a little survey in our bathroom this week and found 12 different colognes or perfumes between Keith and me. That's a little embarrassing, but the alternative would be worse.

We like to smell good, and smelling good has been important for quite some time. History documents perfume back 3500 years. Americans spend billions on perfumes each year...with the most expensive being $31,000 an ounce.

Aromas, in general, play a significant part in our lives. Nothing beats fresh bread or chocolate chip cookies baking in the oven. Certain aromas can bring us to a different place, a different time...a special memory. What fragrances remind you of your childhood? Your teen years?

My Grandmother would always put drops of peppermint oil on a tissue for me to inhale when my stomach was upset, and to this day the scent of peppermint brings me comfort. My mother had a special cedar closet where she stored her fur coat. I loved to sneak in there and touch the softness of the fur, and now, whenever I smell cedar, I think of my mother. Ask someone today what scents remind him or her of home. It makes for interesting conversation.

But, as extravagant as the most expensive perfume, or as warm and comforting as a nostalgic smell, Christ's fragrance is incomparable. He is the Rose of Sharon, the Lily of the Valley.

Have you ever noticed that those who smell the best are the ones who produce a subtle whiff of wonderful? It draws you in, and you find yourself saying, "You smell good." Now I'm an authority on this matter because I work in a small office that often acts as a "fragrance bank." People make deposits and then leave. I have customers who just got off work from the chicken plant or like to conserve water by taking fewer baths. I also have customers who REALLY like their perfume or cologne, and I remember them long after they've gone.

What scent do you leave behind? II Corinthians 2:14-15 tells us that God uses us to spread His knowledge everywhere like a sweet-smelling perfume. Our offering to God is this: We are the sweet smell of Christ among those who are being saved and among those who are being lost. When we draw close to God, we smell like Jesus! The longer we walk with Him, the more welcoming and comforting our fragrance becomes. People want to be around us, and as we share the love of Christ with them, they begin to smell better too. It's a phenomenal marketing and distribution plan.

When you pray today, take some time to bask in the aroma of the One who gave His life for you. Remember His love, His sacrifice. Bathe in His fragrance, and hopefully, as you go about your day, others will see the difference in you and be drawn to the One who made the difference

38

The Voice

No, not the current popular TV show—the voice in our head that suggests maybe you're not headed in the right direction. The one you tend to ignore, because, because...well, that's what I want to talk about. Let's start with a story that, I warn you, is going to make ME look very STUPID.

I had the opportunity to spend an entire day at a spa in New York. I was with Grace, Aryka, and Rachel. A lovely "Girls' Day Out." We enjoyed swimming in the pools, resting in the hot tubs, and even a wonderful neck and shoulder massage. We decided we had time for one more treatment and, since it wasn't very expensive and we could all participate together, we chose a foot and leg massage.

The massage sounded like a wonderful idea seeing as I had been experiencing some bad foot cramps in the preceding days. We entered a large room with a long line of oversized chaise lounges. We were directed to our spots and greeted by our masseuses who apparently didn't speak English. The music was soft and the treatment began.

Within minutes I was experiencing some discomfort (ding). I looked at the other gals. They all seemed to be committed to the luxurious experience so I thought "maybe this painful hot spot is the source of my cramping problem, and this is the therapy I need." I took a deep breath and tried to relax. I had a few moments of relief but then...OUCH!, that kind of hurts (ding).

Before I knew it, my masseuse was lifting my leg as high as he could and then dropping it like a hot potato. That didn't feel so great. He wasn't paying much attention to me, but rather joking with his friends who were working with other clients (ding, ding). Lift and drop, lift and drop.

Geez, I hope this is over soon. Again, I glanced at my gang, and they all seemed fine. I must be a big baby. I told myself to relax, try to enjoy the experience...this is good for you.

Whoa, up in the air goes my leg again, but this time he begins to SLAP it. Yes, I said slap, not pat—holy cow that doesn't feel good (DING). In fact, it really hurts (DING, DING). SLAP! SLAP! SLAP! Oh, let's not forget the other leg—SLAP! SLAP! SLAP! PLEASE STOP! (You would have thought I said out loud), but no...I quietly endured the torture because I thought I was supposed to be enjoying it. After all, everyone else seemed to be enjoying it.

After 20 minutes of torture, he was finished. I paid him. I tipped him...for torturing me—because it was WHAT EVERYBODY ELSE WAS DOING.

Outside of the "therapy" room, I confessed to my girls that I didn't really enjoy the experience; in fact, it actually hurt. Two of the other three quickly chimed in, "IT DID HURT!" After a few seconds of "why didn't you say something?" and "why didn't YOU say something?" we began to laugh at ourselves and realized our foolishness.

There are numerous situations in the world today where we act against our instincts because we try to "fit in." "I should like this because everyone seems to be liking it—it's the cool thing to do—there must be something wrong with me if I don't like this. The voice that says "this isn't good for you" is a voice we need to listen to—despite what the world appears to be shouting.

> *"Does not wisdom shout out? Does not under-standing raise her voice."*
>
> *Proverbs 8:1 NIV*

Call it common sense, call it the Holy Spirit...whatever the source, I disregarded the "dings" and I paid the penalty. I literally had bruises on my legs for the next week. It was a subtle reminder that the world doesn't always know what's good for

ME. The next time you find yourself enduring something that just doesn't feel right, listen to the voice.

You'll save yourself from a lot of bruises.

39

Just a Little Concealer

"On Christ the solid rock I stand, all other ground is sinking sand, all other ground is..."

All I wanted was a concealer that actually worked...you know, cover up the dark circles of death under my eyes and other various flaws. I've been in search of the perfect product since I discovered makeup. It's become even more desperate now that well-meaning people continue to tell me how tired I look. I am forever optimistic that, even though I've tried probably a hundred different products that have been less than successful, there must be something out there that actually works. I just haven't found it yet. So not long ago I purposely walked into a well-known beauty chain store and was met by a young, beautiful makeup artist.

"How can I help you today?" she eagerly asked.

I confidently replied, "Well, I'm looking for a GOOD concealer that..."

"Oh, I can help you with that. I have just the thing—
right this way."

I followed for a few steps, and she instructed me to sit in a chair (that was in the front window facing the street).

"I'll be right back," she said and disappeared.

I thought, "Hmmm, I feel a bit awkward in this window, but I suppose it's a good idea to see the products in natural light. Yes, this is going to go well."

She reappeared with a handful of products (I must have looked extremely tired that day) and asked me a few questions about what I currently use. The next thing I know there's a wet cotton ball swiping my entire face.

"I'll show you the concealer in a minute, but I want to show you something you're going to love," she assured me.

"But, I just wanted..." Oh well, maybe I'm about to discover the product that will be my saving grace. Maybe this woman was created for such a time as this. She is my dark circle savior. Perhaps today is the start of something new...the first day of the rest of my life—I'll never look tired again...and, by the time I finished every positive cliché I could think of, she had eradicated all the makeup from my face except for the dark smudges under my eyes where the mascara had smeared.

And then she said, "Hang on just a minute. I need to help this customer real quick," and she disappeared.

Did I mention I was seated in the front window? People were walking by. People were looking. People were glancing away quickly as if they had just seen a deformity but wanted to be kind enough not to acknowledge it. For a brief moment, I thought about posing as a mannequin, but then it occurred to me that would probably draw more attention. Better to be the pitiful woman with smudgy eyes. Maybe they would pray.

My makeup super hero finally returned and proceeded to slap more makeup on my face than I normally wear in a week. She continually oohed and aahed and pronounced how magnificent I looked, but when she would give me a quick glance into her mirror, I was just confused. Surely this is all going to come together in the end.

She dusted me with bronzer and cheered at her own fabulosity and then said, "Oh wait...the concealer. I like to put that on last. You don't really need very much when you have a good foundation."

How often do we walk into church or Bible study asking for concealer? Just enough Jesus to cover up the mistakes—to make us look and maybe even feel a little better. I don't know about you, but I don't want a little bit of Jesus. I want a Jesus makeover every day of my life. That might mean my life will look a little different than I'm used to, but that's okay—Jesus is a lot more artistic than I am, and when He's done, well, I won't need any concealer at all.

Remember, you don't really need concealer if you have a good foundation. By the way, Keith took me to lunch after my make-over and said he felt like he was out with a different woman—and he liked it. My prayer for you today is that as you get to know Jesus and live by His word people will notice the difference, and they too, will like it!

40

Timing is Everything

"Therefore, if anyone is in Christ, the new creation has come: The old has gone."II Corinthians 5:17

One of the best parts of coming under the Lordship of Jesus Christ is becoming a new creation...the hope of being different...the chance of a new beginning. All things become new!

I had a thought, so I looked up the definition of the word "become." It means "begin to be" or "grow to be." Many new believers grab on to the Bible verse above with the belief that all of their former struggles are gone...vanished, only to be disappointed when temptation comes their way or painful emotions still linger. I have heard many glorious testimonies of immediate deliverance—glory to God, but more often than not, our "becoming a new creation" is a process. However, it's a process with the promise of completion. And that, my friend, gives us HOPE even in the dark times.

I recently had the opportunity to visit Budapest, Hungary, for my nephew Ben and Orsi's wedding. My entire family was there to celebrate. On my first day there, my sister-in-law Mary Ann and her daughter Coreen (who had arrived the day before) told me of an adventure I couldn't pass up. Yes, it was a spa treatment, but one like I'd never had before.

So, the next day I headed to the spa with Cindy, Grace and, yes, even Keith, and I had the experience of little catfish from Thailand eating the dead skin from my feet. I giggle even at the memory. Just to put my feet in the water took faith. Once I took the plunge, just a few bold fish came to inspect what may or may not be worthy of their attention. Evidently I was in the category of prime rib because, within seconds, my tired tourist feet became a bodacious buffet.

It tickled just enough to make you giggle. Occasionally the fish would nibble a little aggressively, but I can't really say it hurt. I was soon comfortable and amazed in my new habitat. I looked forward to my perfectly soft, smooth feet. After about 5 or 10 minutes, I assumed I must be close to showing off my newly groomed dogs, but the attendant explained to me that I must be patient for the best result...30 minutes minimum. Seriously? The attendant kept me occupied by selling me beauty products made from the minerals from the Dead Sea. By now, you know my weakness for beauty products, so let's just say $250.00 later my feet were once again soft and delicate.

The old had become new...but it took time. It took patience. It took unusual tickles and a few bites. It even took some costly (did you catch the $250.00?) mistakes.

Becoming all that God wants you to be is often a process. It takes time. It takes patience. There will be pleasurable times of growth and some rough times. You'll make mistakes.

God is the one who began this good work in you, and I am certain that he won't stop before it is complete." Philippians 1:6

It's a process. Hang in there and, most important, keep your feet in the water.

41

Evolution of My Bath

When I was a child, I typically spent my weekends at Grandma's house, so my initial personal bathing ritual started on Saturday nights in Grandma's tub. I took my Saturday night baths very seriously, covering myself with my "magic" cream. I would rub the bar of soap with bubbles generated by dishwashing liquid until it became a thick lather. I would carefully apply it to my little arms and legs, and as I rinsed it off, I would pretend my skin became magically soft and beautiful. Grandma would come in at some point and scrub my head with Prell shampoo, and since we hadn't discovered conditioner or blow dryers yet, my hair would frizz with delight.

Another highlight of Saturday night baths involved Grandma's Avon products. My Aunt Marie was an Avon representative, and she kept Grandma's shelves well stocked. I was allowed to use her perfumed lotion and dusting powder. I remember slathering and poofing till I was white and the room was cloudy. Cleopatra had nothing over me (well, except for those servants...but I pretended I had those too—good enough). I would slip into a fresh nightgown and settle in for Lawrence Welk, a dance along with Bobby and Sissy, and the Saturday Night movie. Ah, the luxury of it all.

Through my teen years, a luxurious bath always proceeded a school dance, a party or a date. I had now graduated to real bubble bath, Herbal Essence shampoo AND conditioner, and a razor. It was also about this time that my sister Cindy introduced me to egg white facials. These made my face look and feel spectacular. On occasion a bath would also follow a bad experience. A lot of sadness, hurt, disappointment, and anger went down the drain of my tub.

The Saturday morning of my wedding found me in the tub while my sister prepared my favorite breakfast of fried eggs, sausage, and toast. It's no surprise that I would prepare myself for my groom with my favorite ritual, along with the egg white facial. The Avon products were now replaced with Halston perfume and lotion.

The bathtub took on an even more significant meaning when I had children. Now, with the addition of scented candles, it became a respite. I joined the ranks of women who discovered that Calgon really could "take me away." This is when I also discovered bath oil quenching the thirst of my increasingly aging skin.

Another turning point came when we built a new house, complete with a corner tub and two giant windows overlooking the garden and pond. With the children's college education paid for, I now had the resources to invest in some luxury bath products, face masks, and hair treatments. Half-hour baths now became hour-long baths, typically on a late Saturday afternoon. It was about this same time I began hauling the CD player into the bathroom to provide the perfect background music for reminiscing, contemplating, and dreaming as I soaked in splendor.

This brings us to the present. The latest additions have been the world's best foot scrubber, Cherry Merlot soap, and Pandora. (Side note: You will NOT get electrocuted if your blue tooth speaker falls into the tub.) I probably do more reminiscing than dreaming. There's an extra layer of moisturizer, Dead Sea mineral face masks, and self-tanner now. And...I still believe in the magic. I have no idea where my baths will take me in the future. I just hope there are plenty more. What I DO know is that despite all the changes, one thing remains constant:

I still love to slip into a fresh nightgown and settle in for a Saturday night movie. Sorry, Bobby and Sissy, my dance card is full, but I will take another slice of pizza.

If you want a scripture for this...read Leviticus, and you'll discover that a bath is the solution for all sorts of issues!

42

VIB

 *M*ost of us have an obsession or two. I'll admit mine are a bit unusual, but we're not here to judge now, are we? Okay, so I find more enjoyment than most in beauty products. Many years ago when my sister Penny introduced me to Sephora in Seattle, I thought I had found the door to heaven. Not only was the entire store dedicated to beauty products, but I could try anything I liked...and I could even take samples home. I'm a little short of breath even now remembering that day.

Makeup and beauty enhancement is an ancient practice dating back to perhaps even Eve, who thought a little essence of apple could make life a little spicier, but that's a lesson for another day. Cleopatra nailed it, setting eyeliner trends that even the men are picking up on these days. It's the age-old pursuit of being just a bit more attractive that draws us. We make our best effort to cover our flaws, and well, who doesn't like to feel just a little prettier? I will share that I have a secret envy for people who honestly are not concerned with their appearance (life would certainly be simpler), but I honestly AM concerned (that sounded so unspiritual—but hey, we're being honest), so here we are.

Grace emailed me not long ago to share that she had become a "Sephora VIB," proudly announcing that her beauty obsession had finally paid off. She had evidently spent the magical amount of money that promotes you from an average "Beauty Insider" consumer to a VERY IMPORTANT BEAUTY. The title came along with discounts, free shipping, and a total makeover. I laughed at her. I teased her. I may have even tried to shame her a little, but she laughed too, and it was all good. It felt great to know I had been surpassed in the arena of beauty addiction.

A few weeks later, Keith and I were doing our Christmas shopping, and I went into Sephora to make some stocking stuffer purchases (okay, and a get a little something—something for moi). I proudly handed over my "Beauty Insider" card to get a few extra samples, and that's when the cashier announced rather loudly: "CONGRATULATIONS, YOU JUST HIT VIB STATUS." Frankly, I was a little embarrassed. I looked at the other customers who were looking at me. I saw looks of approval, envy, and I'm pretty sure one lady was sneering in disgust. Oh, how I missed Grace at the moment—looks like we're on even ground again.

So TODAY, I can, with confidence in my VIB credentials, tell you that I have discovered the most outstanding method of bringing the "perfect glow" to your complexion. You may be too "oily" and have been searching for the ideal matte powder that keeps you looking natural. Or you may be dry and a little wrinkled, desperate for the right amount of hydration to restore that supple, youthful softness. Pay attention, I have something "outside of ordinary" for you to consider:

Recently my friend Katie sent her usual encouragement text and quoted Psalm 34:5:

"Those who look to Him are radiant, and their faces shall never be ashamed."

Then she reminded me of when Moses came down from the mountain, his face shone from being in the presence of God (Exodus 34:29)

And my favorite one:

"So our faces are not covered, they show the bright glory of the Lord, as the Lord's Spirit makes us more and more like our glorious Lord."

II Corinthians 3:18

I truly hope and pray the Spirit of the Lord shines through you and me (and all our beauty products) every day. The best news is: we don't have to spend way too much money at Sephora, we've already achieved VIB status with God—no purchase necessary.

Oh, and the perks? He's paid the entire price for our salvation (John 3:16), He promises an abundant life (John 10:10), and his makeover is EXTRAORDINARY!

> *"Anyone who belongs to Christ is a new person. The past is forgotten, and everything is new.*
>
> *II Cor 5:17 CEV*

Outside
of
Ordinary
Reflections

43

Habitudes

We all resolve to be better, to do better, but it's often harder than we think. As part of my New Year's resolutions, this year I decided I needed to let go of my word puzzle game. Yes, I am an addict. I revert to my word puzzle whenever I have downtime. I've always justified that it was good for my brain, but even as I play, I can feel the addictive spirit all over me—I always just want to play "one more round." And to make matters worse, I often feel if I *don't* have time to play, I feel like I am being deprived of "real" relaxation. Here's my dilemma: I know I could be using my time more profitably even while relaxing with my iPad. I could read, for example, which would give me a break from my reality but prove a source for some further education. And, since I chose KNOWLEDGE as my word of 2017, therein lies a perfect source. So, instead of playing my word puzzle game, I chose to travel around the world with three girls in a really fun novel, "The Lost Girls." I learned about the Amazon and life in a hostel. We hiked to Machu Picchu and dared to go into the slums of Rio. We worked at a school for girls in Africa, we...well, you'll just have to pick up a copy for yourself, but let me finish by saying New Zealand is now on my real-life bucket list.

Resolving to be better does not have to be painful—it's simply a matter of adjusting your HABITUDES...the patterns of what you think or feel. In this instance, playing my word puzzle was what I thought brought me comfort and/or joy. Somewhere along the line I equated relaxation with the game, and it became a habit. When I challenged my thinking (attitude) and dared to try something different, I found a much better source of comfort. And to think I was trapped in problem-solving when I could have been traveling the world and meeting new people.

I challenge you to consider a different perspective, change it up, and find the adventure that awaits. Who knows, maybe some of you who are stuck in a book should try a word game!

Beware of the habitudes—they can steal your joy as well as the potential for so much more. There's a lotta life out there to be lived...step out of your circle of ordinary and explore the adventure.

As I'm reading through the Bible this year (another resolution), I am gaining new insights and even more knowledge of all that God has to offer. I forgot how wonderful the Old Testament stories are and how encouraging a Psalm can be in the midst of the frustrations of life:

"I praise you, Lord, for being my guide. Even in the darkest night, your teachings fill my mind. I will always look to you, as you stand beside me, and protect me from fear. With all my heart, I will celebrate, and I can safely rest."

Psalm 16:7-9

...and who doesn't love a reason to celebrate!

44

Why I Go to Church

When I was a child, I went to church because that's what you were supposed to do on Sunday mornings. It was part of my religion. When I was a teenager, my Mom gave me a choice, so I stopped going for a short while...it seemed rebellious, which seemed cool at the time. When my life became hard, I went back to church, hoping God would see my action and make my life better. When I realized my need for a savior and surrendered my life to Jesus, I went to church to understand this new relationship.

In today's culture, it is not necessary to physically attend church to learn or even to worship. You can just watch it online, you can pay your tithe online, you can even get other stuff done around the house while listening to the sermon or singing along with the songs. I am grateful for the technology that can bring the experience of church into our homes, really I am...but,

Here's why I *go* to church:

- I LOVE singing and worshipping with others. I love to feel the presence of God as we lift our voices in praise.
- I LOVE hugging my friends, encouraging them through their struggles, and having them encourage me as well.
- I LOVE the opportunity to use my gifts to teach others, serve others, and make a difference.
- I LOVE being challenged by the message each Sunday and having the opportunity to pray with others.
- I LOVE to go to church as an offering of my time to Jesus. I take the time to celebrate His love, to further that love, and to share that love with my brothers and sisters.

The church is a community, and community is so important. We all need to be part of something. The church is an exchange of life's best gifts: faith, hope, and love. It's an opportunity to grow, to be better, and to be used by God.

I Corinthians 12 tells us that we each have something unique to bring to the table. Your church *needs* you to be complete!

"Whenever two or three of you come together in my name, I am there with you." Matthew 18:20

"Some people have given up the habit of meeting for worship, but we must not do that. We should keep on encouraging each other, especially since

you know that the day of the Lord's coming is get-
ting closer." Hebrews 10:25

Find a church that's right for you. Don't go to church because you're supposed to...go to church to experience all God has for you...

It's an extraordinary place to be!

45

Gold Medal Life

"So we must get rid of everything that slows us down, especially the sin that just won't let go. And we must be determined to run the race that is ahead of us."

Hebrews 12:1

"The scriptures train God's people to do all kinds of good deeds"

II Timothy 3:17

Every two years we have the thrill of watching the world's best athletes compete in the Olympics. I really enjoy watching the various competitions. Gymnastics is my favorite by far. I cannot help but be continually amazed and inspired by the discipline of the athletes no matter what sport I am watching. They dedicate their *life* to their sport with the intention of becoming *the best.*

No one would take them seriously, nor would they experience much success if they casually worked out and "hoped" they would do well if ever tested. Imagine a gymnast training with a casual mentality:

"I did that triple twisting flip really well last Friday. Glad I accomplished that. Hopefully I can do it again at the Olympics."

I think of the gymnast, Aly Raisman. She made the decision to come back after the 2012 Olympics to compete again in the 2016 Olympics. When she showed up at the gym, her coach would not even look at her until he was convinced she was truly "all in." It's no surprise that to become an Olympic athlete one has to be dedicated, sincere, and willing to do more than expected or even desired. One has to practice every day, all day, and then some more. I doubt they ever walk away from a practice thinking, "I got this, I don't need to practice again."

So, we get it, we're impressed, and we applaud their efforts and successes. BUT...here's my thought: what if we applied the Olympic attitude and discipline to our spiritual life? I think it's easy to illustrate the casual attitude:

- I might go to church, if my schedule allows.
- I read through the Bible once, so I have a pretty good idea what it says.
- I believe in God.
- I try to be a good person, but hey, nobody's perfect.

- I give money to worthy causes when I have some extra.
- Two years ago, I filled in for a Sunday School teacher.
- You fill in the rest.

I hesitate to make a similar list for a disciplined walk with God only because a "gold medal" walk is a matter of the heart and soul. It is drenched in God's grace and mercy...it is NOT a to-do list or a list of rules—because face it, we will never be good enough through our own efforts. We all know where we, as individuals, fall short and when our practice, training, and discipline are "less than." I'd rather let the Holy Spirit guide you (He's a little more qualified). I want to inspire you today to take a look at your own life...I want to motivate you to do better, to be better. Step out of your circle of ordinary and strive for an extraordinary life, dedicated to pleasing God and being used by God to make a difference in your world. It may take a little more discipline and practice. It's definitely a daily choice, and it goes way beyond the walls of your church. It shows up in your family, your workplace, your conversations, your attitudes, and your decisions. And, it REALLY helps to know the ins and outs, so be sure to study the manual. Why settle for mediocrity when you can:

GO FOR THE GOLD!

46

The Window

"You will see His kingdom reaching far and wide."

Isaiah 33:17 CEV

For two years my sister Cindy lived in a studio apartment in Chicago that only had one window, and that one window faced a wall. She could not even see the ground to know if it had snowed. She lived there comfortably, thankful for her home.

The day arrived when she moved into a new apartment that had a large window looking out over Lake Michigan. She could see several buildings, a golf course, some tennis courts, and best of all, the horizon. The view was the primary reason she chose her new habitat; well, that and the fact it was actually lower rent and had a swimming pool.

The really interesting part of the story is that during the first few days in her new space she felt "unbalanced." The expanse of her view was a little unsettling. She realized she lost a sense of security when her world opened up.

That happens when we step out of "ordinary." The world can feel a little scary...a new perspective can challenge what previously felt "safe." But once we regain our balance, we realize there is so much more to see. There's a part of life we never experienced before. We reinvent our "normal."

On Cindy's first day she took in her view and noticed a wedding taking place. Much to her surprise (since she thought her building faced north), she saw the first of many beautiful sunsets to come. Who knew?

The next big surprise was that her new apartment provided cable service. So after two years of viewing only Netflix, she discovered she had 100 channels from which to choose. She was so overwhelmed that she just turned to Netflix.

Baby steps.

47

Thanks, Pillsbury

For me, Thanksgiving is about preparing a day of warm celebration for my family. My favorite ones have been in my own home, and trust me, they are steeped in tradition. For example, I like to start the day with a special breakfast of "hot rolls." Now, before you think I'm kneading dough and creating a homemade delicacy, I'll let you in on the family secret: I'm talking about those Pillsbury cinnamon rolls that come in the tube in your local dairy case. I make them once a year, but they reflect years and years of family memories for me:

> *"HOT ROLLS!" my mother would yell, and my siblings and I would jump out of bed, race to the kitchen table, and just hope we would be the one to get the gooiest cinnamon roll strategically located in the center of the round pan.*

My children and husband don't really grasp the sentiment of the Thanksgiving morning cinnamon rolls, but it puts a huge smile in my heart. Now, if the time works out, my family is enjoying their "hot rolls" while watching the Macy's Parade. To be honest, I don't really care if I watch the parade, but I love to hear the sound of it in the background while I start making preparations for the traditional meal...it's simply the sound of Thanksgiving. Over the years, a new tradition has developed in our household: a battle over watching the dog show or the football game after the parade. I vote dog show.

But let's get to dinner: We always have turkey, but I have experimented with different ways of preparing the bird over the years. There was roasting, bagging, and brining. I have settled for the turkey roaster for the last few years (with great success I might add). The important and fun thing to know about the turkey in our house isn't the method of cooking—it's all about the name. I usually have the honor of naming the turkey each year, but I'm always open for suggestions. The turkey is named after the one person, outside of our immediate family, who was the biggest turkey—affecting our family in a negative way. As I write this, I realize how juvenile this sounds, but it is so satisfying to close the oven door (or drop the roasting pan lid) on that turkey after a long year of frustration! We keep a list of all turkey names, and it includes ex-boyfriends, girlfriends, employers, co-workers—well, you get the picture. The list, by the way, is kept in a very secret place, only to be reviewed at the Thanksgiving table each year. It's a great conversation starter.

SOOOOO, along with our traditional turkey, we always have mashed potatoes, gravy, stuffing, green bean casserole, sweet potatoes, cranberries, pumpkin pie, and an absolute must—CRESCENT ROLLS. Now I am not a dairy case kind of girl, really I'm not, but it's the story of the CRESCENT ROLLS that keeps me coming back each year. In addition to the above-listed usual fare, I always try to bring something new to the table. The only food that has stuck and become a tradition is my homemade cranberries that replaced my Mom's traditional canned cranberries. She would present them freshly "slid" from the can on a crystal serving dish (still shaped like a can with the indentations in the middle—she thought it was pretty). Anyway, let's get back to the CRESCENT ROLLS and what has become a favorite family tradition:

This tradition takes place with all my siblings, whether we're together or not. Please note that if we are apart, we call each other and report in. So what must happen at the end of the Thanksgiving meal is that a poll must be taken of what was the favorite "taste on the plate." Everyone's response is recorded, and the winning taste is posted in an ongoing log book. It's a delight to hear that the mashed potatoes won in Illinois while the stuffing took the honors in Oklahoma. A bacon-wrapped turkey got an honorable mention in Kansas a few years back.

Now, lest you think I've forgotten about the CRESCENT ROLLS, let's go back about 25 years. My family was sitting around the table after an incredible spread of food. Keep in mind that, like most families, we went all out with side dishes, so picking your favorite taste was even more of a challenge. This particular year, my niece, Lecia brought her boyfriend to dinner. Mary Ann had prepared the majority of the meal (cooking for days), and she did a fabulous job. As the family went around the table, different responses to the "favorite taste" were heard: "turkey," "pistachio salad," "mashed potatoes," you get the picture. And with every response, Mary Ann's smile of satisfaction got wider, until it was "the boyfriend's" turn. He proudly declared the Pillsbury CRESCENT ROLLS to be his very favorite taste. Mic drop. And that is why we continue to have CRESCENT ROLLS every Thanksgiving—to remember the biggest "Turkey of the Year" and have a good chuckle.

By the way, we never saw "the boyfriend" again, bless his heart.

48

Evacuation

*N*ot long ago I had the opportunity to go to an "Escape Room," where you're given one hour to decipher the clues provided (if you can find the clues) to open the door in order to exit the room. On this particular day we had three groups of family members who were competing against each other. I was excited to have a group of really smart people: a lawyer, a senator, and a science teacher (sounds like the beginning of a good joke). I thought it would be a breeze.

I was immediately overwhelmed when I entered the room, noting that it was "science" oriented—not my forte. There were eight combination locks plus a brief case that was locked—all of which held the clues, plus a lot of science stuff.

When I think about this adventure, I quickly see a parallel to life in general:

- It's easy to feel stuck in a situation, wonder if you're ever going to get out or be able to move on. To be successful at getting out, sometimes you have to be willing to dig and explore for the help you need.

- Sometimes in all this "digging" you make it harder than it needs to be. I was notorious for this in our escape room. Maybe it's my creative mind, but I kept getting distracted by these symbols I found and thought they meant something—when the real answers were right in front of me.
- I found myself frustrated—the number of locks seemed daunting. I could hear the cheers of the teams in the other room when they would get something unlocked. So unfair!
- The successes came when we collaborated, and often that meant seeing the clues from someone else's perspective;

It holds true in our daily lives. Sometimes the answers we need are right in front of us, but we simply need a different light shone on them:

- advice from a friend
- truth from the Word of God
- maybe just breathing and focusing on the immediate problem instead of the bigger picture

"Your word is a lamp that given light wherever I walk." Psalm 199:105

When we're stuck, He shows us the way.

I'll be honest with you, we did not escape the room that day—we failed. But guess what? We actually still got out, because obviously the staff came in and rescued us. This is actually the best news of all because we DO sometimes fail, but God never does—He's always there to rescue us no matter how stuck we are.

Wow!—so many lessons learned in the one hour...

...and here I thought I was just going to prove my brilliance.

49

Eyes Wide Open

$\mathcal{I}$ am preparing for another European adventure with my siblings. We're headed to Lithuania to learn about our heritage. I have accepted the responsibility of planning our itinerary. So how do you do that successfully without having ever been to the destination? I have been reading a borrowed travel book and combing the internet for as much information as I can gather. I want to get off that plane and not only have a plan but also an inclination of how things operate in Lithuania...at least a naïve perspective on the culture. I want to be enlightened as opposed to being totally in the dark and having to struggle with navigation.

> *"I ask the glorious Father and God of our Lord Jesus*
> *Christ to give you his Spirit. The Spirit will make*
> *you wise and let you understand what it means to*
> *know God. My prayer is that light will flood your*

hearts and you will understand the hope given to you when God chose you."

Ephesians 1:17-18

This is a letter from Paul to a church, to a group of people he cares about, to a group of people he wants to see grow in their faith. I love this prayer because it shows the process for a fulfilling walk with God. If you need a "tutorial," this prayer is for you!

When we read our Bibles, listen to teachings, attend Bible studies, fellowship with our friends, and attend worship services, we obtain wisdom. I love Oprah's perspective: "When you know better, you do better."

Wisdom opens the doors for us to understand the truth of who God is. His promises for us are revealed. Our lives are affected, we are simply different when our hearts are full of truth. When we live in truth, it changes our perspective. The eyes of our heart are enlightened, and when our hearts see through the lenses of truth, we see HOPE. There's hope for the difficult situation you are facing right now, there's hope for your children, there's hope for today, and there's always hope for tomorrow. When our hearts are full of truth, we know who we are and where we are going.

I know what mode of transportation to take when I arrive in Vilnius. I know how to get to my hotel. I am familiar with the sights I want to see. I know how long it will take me to drive from one city to another, and I know a little bit about the culture. I have knowledge, and my eyes are open. I won't have to waste time learning off the cuff or recovering from senseless mistakes. I will be prepared, and that will give me the opportunity to enjoy the surprises and adventures that await. I also know the time and date of my flight home to my husband and children.

So step out of your circle, and prepare yourself for your journey ahead. There will be tough days and unforeseen surprises, but in the midst of the struggle, always remember:

You're headed home.

50

Head Shots

"Act like people with good sense and not like fools. These are evil times, so make every minute count. Don't be stupid. Instead, find out what the Lord wants you to do."

Ephesians 15-17

*Y*ou know how sometimes you want something so desperately you fixate on it, you lose all common sense, and you are determined to do whatever it takes to get "it"? I was recently reminded of a time long ago, when I was pregnant with Joel, I was with my friend who was even a little more pregnant and my sister-in-law Kathie who was "pregnant enough." The three of us piled into Kathie's sleek suburban (she was "pregnant enough" with her fourth child, and her vehicle said it all). We were driving down Main Street on a warm summer morning, and we pulled up to a stoplight. Lo and behold, a vehicle of young men pulled up right next to us. They noticed the three young girls in the sleek suburban. Now I mentioned that we were all pregnant, but we were also all young, blonde, and well, cute. The men began to honk, wave, and carry on. Even more pregnant than me, Mary said, "We should really mess with these guys." Of course, I stated that would not be the Godly thing to do—okay, I didn't say that. Instead, we rolled down our windows and giggled and flirted with boys. The light turned green, and we were off, laughing and enjoying our antics. A few blocks later we turned into the parking lot of our destination, and sure enough, that vehicle of young men was right behind us. They pulled up right next to our ever so sleek Suburban. Now we're really laughing. So we smile a little more, and we waved a little more, and then we slowly opened the doors and slithered our voluptuous bellies out the vehicle and waddled over to their car.

"Hey guys!"

I didn't know eyes could get that big. In a flash we went from "girls" to "ladies" as the driver pronounced, "Hey ladies, have a nice day," and drove off.

Lesson learned: Be cautious when you begin to pursue something with great determination. Whether it be a position, a relationship, power, fame, a new pair of shoes, or even a piece of cake, you might only be getting a "head shot." You don't have a clue regarding the burdens and responsibilities that go with the bigger picture.

Sometimes the smartest thing you can do is smile and keep on driving.

51

A Recycled Moment

From as early as I can remember, I wanted to get married. I couldn't imagine anything more magical than my very own wedding: the beautiful dress, a day of celebration, but most important, a groom, a man who loved ME. I spent so much time dreaming of my special day that when Keith proposed to me, it only took me a week to plan the wedding. It was just a matter of placing a few phone calls...the venue, the florist, the caterer, the printer, and the photographer. Done! I bought the dress the next week and ordered the tuxes, lined up the musicians, set the rehearsal...let's go! Why is this so hard for people? Perhaps this is why I ended up working as a wedding coordinator years down the line. I was born for weddings.

As weeks went by, I polished every detail I could dream. I played it over and over again in my head. It would be the perfect day. And it truly was—because the few snags that may have occurred had no bearing on the one moment that I had envisioned, and that moment was everything I had hoped for. Let me take you there.

My bridesmaids left me to begin the processional. I was alone. Most brides are with their fathers at this point, but I made a unique decision to have my father meet me as I came down the aisle. I chose to spend those last minutes as a single woman with Jesus, and it was very special to me. When the time was right, I climbed the two flights of stairs that would take me to the chapel.

The ushers were instructed to have the two large wooden doors to the sanctuary closed so my groom would not see me. I positioned myself with the sun streaming thru the large stained glass window behind me (it's all in the staging and lighting—why I ended up directing plays later on in life—I was born for drama). The song I had carefully chosen, "This is The Day" by Scott Wesley Brown, was being played by the pianist who began to take it to a crescendo with a carefully orchestrated fanfare, and then the doors were pulled open revealing the bride to the groom and the groom to the bride. Other than seeing my waiting father weeping, there was no distraction between the bride and the groom. My face was set forward, and my only intention was to get to the end of the aisle where the one I loved most was waiting with the most beautiful smile I had ever seen.

That happened 36 years ago. I remember falling asleep that night thinking I'd accomplished my life's dream; it's all downhill from here. Little did I know all of the joys that were still to come: the birth of our children, personal accomplishments, and great adventures.

As I continue to check dreams and goals off my bucket list, I now dream of the day when I will, once again, find myself alone. I will be done climbing the steps. I will be more than ready to take my position. The gates will open, and my eyes will meet the eyes of my Savior. My face will be set forward, and my only intention will be to run into the arms of the One who loves me most.

Who knows? Maybe Scott Wesley Brown will even be singing "This is The Day."

52

The Sack Lunch

I recently read the story in the Bible about the little boy who gave his lunch to Jesus, and Jesus in turn fed the 5000. One of my favorite ways to read the stories in the gospels is to look "behind the scenes" and imagine the back story. In this instance I thought about the mother who packed that boy's lunch. Perhaps throwing those two fish and those loaves of bread into the sack was just another mundane chore for her. I wonder if she was just plain tired of meeting everyone else's needs. I wonder who caught those two fish?—maybe the boy's father? Maybe they were purchased from a nearby fisherman... just another mundane chore. I wonder if the boy whined at the idea of having to carry around a sack lunch all day (apparently it wasn't the cool thing to do since none of the other 4999 plus didn't carry one)—how embarrassing.

Have you ever noticed that miracles often start with the mundane? When Jesus performed miracles, He didn't start with spectacular, He didn't:

- make sure the lighting was correct;
- have the perfect background music;
- choose the most talented or best-looking people;
- market so He got more "likes." (In fact, I remember a particular miracle where He asked that they tell no one, hmmm.)

Jesus was all about taking the ordinary and making it extraordinary:

- water into wine;
- blindness into sight;
- lame into dancing;
- a sack lunch into an all-you-can- eat buffet;
- death into life.

THE GOD OF THE UNEXPECTED!

I think about my friend Jill. She had the idea of giving bracelets to all the women who attended our BRAVE conference. She immediately volunteered to take on the task of designing and acquiring the BRAVE bracelets. I never heard much about it after that, but sure enough, every woman who walked through those doors was given a bracelet. Nice touch, right? So weeks later a story comes my way of a young woman who attended the conference. She found herself at a Bible study and felt she should share her testimony. The only problem being that she didn't really *want* to speak up. She would rather just sit back and listen. It was then that she looked down and saw her BRAVE bracelet. She mustered up the courage to speak. Afterwards four separate women thanked her for her message that encouraged them. Another story followed of a bracelet given to a young mother at the funeral of her two- month-old baby. Jill's obedience to her task changed lives.

The scripture tells us that when Jesus took that sack lunch, He lifted it up and gave thanks...and then the feast began. The next time you are caught in the middle of "mundane," remember the woman who packed the lunch that day and lift up your sack of "ordinary life," give thanks, and watch what God can do.

Any day can be extraordinary when you step out-side your circle of expectation!

Special Thanks to:

My Husband, for putting up with my MANY projects and loving me unconditionally;

My children, Joel and Grace, for providing much of the material... you are loved more than you will ever know;

Margery Warder and Wayne Shaw who said, "You should write a book." Even more thanks to Margery for the assistance in writing and publishing;

Penny for her editing expertise and encouragement;

Linda Galbraith – my editor who became my friend and a wonderful supporter

Cindy, Rachel, and Celeste who actually believed I could do this— let's always celebrate each other!

Lori Klickman would love to share her stories at your next event.

Please contact her at:

Outsideofordinary.Lori@gmail.com

Visit her website at outsideofordinary.org